D1329518

THE
BACKLASH

This book is dedicated to the Sierra Health Foundation of Sacramento, California. The Foundation provided essential financial support for a conference on the backlash, held in Sacramento in November 1992.

*This book is also dedicated to kids—
all of them, but especially my own, Eric and Willie.*

THE BACKLASH

Child Protection Under Fire

John E. B. Myers

editor

SAGE Publications
International Educational and Professional Publisher
Thousand Oaks   London   New Delhi

For information address:

 SAGE Publications, Inc.
2455 Teller Road
Thousand Oaks, California 91320

SAGE Publications Ltd.
6 Bonhill Street
London EC2A 4PU
United Kingdom

SAGE Publications India Pvt. Ltd.
M-32 Market
Greater Kailash I
New Delhi 110048 India

Printed in the United States of America

Library of Congress Cataloging-in-Publication Data

Main entry under title:

The backlash: Child protection under fire/ edited by John E. B. Myers.
p. cm.
Includes bibliographical references and index.
ISBN 0-8039-5403-4 (cl.)—ISBN 0-8039-5404-2 (pbk.)
1. Social work with children—United States. 2. Abused children—Services for —United States. 3. Child abuse—United States.
I. Myers, John E. B.
HV741.B26   1994   94-10881
362.7'0973—dc20   CIP

95 96 97 10 9 8 7 6 5 4 3 2

Sage Production Editor: Yvonne Könneker

Contents

Acknowledgments

Many people created this book. Special thanks go to the professionals who attended a conference on the backlash, held at the University of the Pacific, McGeorge School of Law, in November 1992. These professionals are named in the Introduction. I also want to express appreciation to the Sierra Health Foundation of Sacramento, California, which provided financial support for the conference. Finally, I owe a debt of gratitude to the many professionals and parents around the country who sent me information on the backlash in their communities.

Introduction

In 1988, David Hechler published *The Battle and the Backlash: The Child Sexual Abuse War.* Hechler describes the battle being waged to force society to recognize child sexual abuse as a serious problem. Hechler (1988) also describes the backlash against such recognition, writing:

> One thing is clear; there *is* a war. There are those who feel that the country is suffering from an epidemic of child sexual abuse and those who feel that there is an epidemic all right, but not of sex abuse—of "sex accuse," as some have disparagingly called it. The pendulum has swung too far, they say, and what we see now is a blizzard of false accusations. (p. 3)

Six years have elapsed since the publication of *The Battle and the Backlash.* Yet the battle is far from over. Indeed, the conflict has intensified. The time is ripe for a new "report from the front." Where are we today? Who is winning? Are the child protection forces moving ahead? Or is the backlash gaining ground?

To begin answering these questions, an invitational conference was held at the University of the Pacific, McGeorge School of Law, in Sacramento, California, on November 20 and 21, 1992. The conference was titled Defining and Responding to the Backlash Against Child Protection, and was made possible with a grant from the Sierra Health Foundation of Sacramento. The Sierra Health Foundation is an independent foundation committed to supporting health-related activities in Northern California. The present vol-

ume grew out of the papers presented and the recommendations
made at this conference. The following individuals attended the
conference:

Sandra Baker, M.S.W.
Director, Child and Family Institute
Sacramento, CA

Lucy Berliner, M.S.W.
Director of Research
Sexual Assault Center
Harborview Medical Center
Seattle, WA

David Chadwick, M.D.
Director, Child Protection Center
Children's Hospital
San Diego, CA

Jon Conte, Ph.D.
Social Work School
University of Washington
Seattle, WA

David Corwin, M.D.
Department of Psychiatry
Washington University Medical School
St. Louis, MO

Howard A. Davidson, J.D.
Director, American Bar Association Center on Children and the Law
Washington, DC

Michael Durfee, M.D.
Director, Child Abuse Prevention Program
Los Angeles County Department of Health Services
Los Angeles, CA

Judge Leonard Edwards
Presiding Judge of the Juvenile Court
San Jose, CA

Robert Fellmeth, J.D.
Director, Children's Advocacy Institute
University of San Diego School of Law
San Diego, CA

David Finkelhor, Ph.D.
Co-Director, Family Research Laboratory
University of New Hampshire
Durham, NH

Gail S. Goodman, Ph.D.
Department of Psychology
University of California, Davis
Davis, CA

Jennifer J. Freyd, Ph.D.
Department of Psychology
University of Oregon
Eugene, OR

Kee MacFarlane, M.S.W.
Director of Resource Development
Children's Institute International
Los Angeles, CA

John E. B. Myers, J.D.
University of the Pacific
McGeorge School of Law
Sacramento, CA

Sylvia Pizzini, M.S.W., M.P.A.
Former Director, Department of Family and Children's Services
Santa Clara County Social Services
San Jose, CA

Inger Sagatum-Edwards, Ph.D.
Administration of Justice Department
San Jose State University
San Jose, CA

Roland C. Summit, M.D.
Department of Psychiatry
Harbor/UCLA Medical Center
Torrance, CA

Donna Terman, J.D.
Center for the Future of Children
The David and Lucile Packard Foundation
Los Altos, CA

Deanne Tilton
Director, Los Angeles County Inter-Agency Council on Child Abuse
   and Neglect
Los Angeles, CA

Patricia Toth, J.D.
Director, National Center for Prosecution of Child Abuse
Alexandria, VA

Lesley Wimberly
President, National Association of State VOCAL Organizations
Sacramento, CA

George Wimberly
Victims of Child Abuse Laws
Sacramento, CA

In Chapter 1, David Finkelhor analyzes the backlash from the perspective of sociological theory of social movements. Finkelhor describes the emergence of child protection as a social movement supported by the women's movement and professionals concerned about child maltreatment. Finkelhor discusses the symbolic value of caring for children as one important factor supporting the child protection movement. Next, Finkelhor dissects the anatomy of the backlash, analyzing its strengths and weaknesses. Finally, Finkelhor offers his outlook for the child protection movement and the backlash.

In Chapter 2, I attempt to define the origins of the backlash. I begin with a brief historical review of child protection as it emerged in the 19th century. Looking back in time, one quickly realizes that child protection has always been criticized. Indeed, criticism is inevitable. Next, I identify three sources of the backlash. First, the emotionality aroused by child abuse fuels polarization and backlash. Second, child abuse is so tragic and unpleasant that society has a tendency to ignore it—as if failure to see it could "make it go away." I examine the historical tendency to suppress recognition of child abuse and to discredit its victims. Third, I take a frank look at the faults of the child protection system and assert that professionals are to blame for much of the backlash.

In Chapter 3, Sylvia Pizzini offers a view of the backlash from the perspective of a county child protective services (CPS) administrator. Pizzini describes the legislative framework of the U.S. child protection system, beginning with the Social Security Act of 1935 and working forward to the Adoption Assistance and Child Welfare Act of 1980. Pizzini outlines the value conflicts and inconsistencies inherent in the laws governing child protection. These conflicts and inconsistencies account in considerable measure for the difficulty experienced in implementing effective protective services for children. Pizzini goes on to describe the many checks and balances built into the child protection system. Finally, Pizzini outlines practical steps for CPS administrators to respond to criticism.

Chapter 4 is by Lesley Wimberly, who is the president of the National Association of State VOCAL Organizations. Wimberly offers the perspective of Victims of Child Abuse Laws (VOCAL)—VOCAL is one of child protection's most persistent and outspoken critics. Anyone wishing to understand the backlash should read Wimberly's chapter carefully. Although most readers of this book will disagree with some of Wimberly's views, it is critically important to understand VOCAL's perspective and to appreciate where VOCAL members are coming from. For too long, some of us in child protection ignored VOCAL and other critics.

Chapter 5 is written by Charles Wilson and Susan Caylor Steppe. Wilson and Steppe describe the backlash from the perspective of state-level CPS administrators. The authors begin by outlining the common elements—and common problems—of CPS agencies. For example, Wilson and Steppe describe the difficulty of attracting sufficient numbers of competent professionals to CPS. The authors go on to define and analyze six criticisms commonly leveled against CPS: (a) CPS accepts anonymous reports and does not adequately screen reports, (b) CPS confuses poverty with neglect, (c) CPS has too much power, (d) CPS staff is not equipped to do the job, (e) reporting laws encourage frivolous reports, and (f) there is a lack of due process protection for individuals whose names are in child abuse registries. Wilson and Steppe's analysis is stimulating because they don't make excuses for CPS. On the contrary, they fully acknowledge the many problems plaguing CPS. Nevertheless, Wilson and Steppe also point out the many successes of CPS, and they conclude with useful recommendations to improve CPS and respond to the backlash.

In Chapter 6, Karel Pyck describes the backlash in Europe. This chapter is interesting for U.S. readers, many of whom know relatively little about the backlash on the other side of the Atlantic. The chapter opens with a brief description of troublesome cases in England, Scotland, Wales, and Belgium. Next, Pyck offers a detailed chronological analysis of one high-profile investigation from the Netherlands. The case arose in the small city of Oude Pekela and involved allegations by many children of sexual abuse by strangers. The investigation drew tremendous media attention, and Pyck's description of events is interesting and informative. Pyck ends his chapter with several lessons from Oude Pekela—lessons that apply in America as well as Europe.

In Chapter 7, I analyze the literature of the backlash. Reviewing numerous magazines, newspapers, television programs, and journals shows constant repetition of the following themes and images: (a) the child protection system is out of control; (b) child protection is a witch-hunt; (c) there is mass hysteria about child abuse; (d) professionals are comparable to Nazis, McCarthyite persecutors, the KGB, and other symbols of evil; and (d) professionals are the cause of problems in child protection. These themes and images are discussed and illustrated with quotes from the literature of the backlash.

In addition to describing common themes of the backlash literature, I point out the rhetorical devices used by critics to bolster their arguments. The chapter ends with recommendations for responding to the literature of the backlash.

Chapter 8 contains a number of recommendations for responding to the backlash. The entire book is laced with recommendations, and I do not restate them all, but rather expand on several recommendations contained in earlier chapters and advance several ideas that do not appear elsewhere.

The backlash is a serious problem, and it is getting worse. I hope this book stimulates debate about the backlash and about ways to improve our beleaguered child protection system.

JOHN E. B. MYERS

ONE

The "Backlash" and the Future of Child Protection Advocacy

Insights From the Study of Social Issues

DAVID FINKELHOR

Child advocates are alarmed. In the late 1980s, after a period of almost exclusively favorable media attention, child protection became more publicly controversial. Politicians accused advocates of over-dramatizing the problem. Attorneys accused them of brainwashing children. Parents who believed themselves to be the victims of child abuse investigations organized to lobby for new restrictive legislation. An opposition, or backlash, against child protection had formed.

Such developments, although surprising to child advocates, were not unpredictable or unprecedented. Sociologists have long noted that social movements engender backlash. Social movements all seem to travel through certain predictable cycles of attention and controversy. They have a "natural history." It begins in the competition for public attention, as hundreds of potential social issues strive for the limelight, with only certain ones emerging successfully into the public arena (Blumer, 1971; Spector & Kitsuse, 1977). Then interest grows, definitions of problems change, opposition comes and goes, coalitions splinter, attention flags, and eventually other problems come to the fore (Downs, 1972; Hilgartner & Bosk, 1988). There are many expected patterns in these changes.

The branch of sociology that studies these matters is called social problems analysis. Those concerned about the problem of child abuse and the backlash can benefit from its insights, and in this chapter, I will try to make some of them available. The analysis needs to start with the social origins and social bases of interest in child abuse. Then a similar analysis will be made of the backlash. Finally, I will try to assess where things might be headed, depending on how these forces interact and develop.

The Social Movement Around Child Abuse

A first principle of social problems analysis is this: Social problems have to be understood as products of social movements (Mauss, 1975). They have to be understood as political phenomena, the results of the interplay of power and influence among groups and operants (Zald & Ash, 1966). In addition, they can be understood symbolically as statements and reflections of psychological conflicts and striving shared by segments of the society and projected onto some particular goals and activities (Blumer, 1971).

By most sociological standards, the mobilizations around child abuse in the 1960s and 1970s, and the related mobilization around sexual abuse in the 1980s, were very successful social problem mobilizations (Nelson, 1984; Pfohl, 1977). That is, compared to other social problem mobilizations, they reached a large audience and galvanized a great deal of professional and public policy activity. By any standards, child abuse and sexual abuse have clearly arrived on the public agenda. They have captured an enormous wave of public attention. All the media have focused on them extensively. Surveys have consistently shown that people are knowledgeable and concerned (Finkelhor, Hotaling, Lewis, & Smith, 1989; Schulman, Ronca, and Bucuvalas, Inc., 1988). A great deal of government and professional activity has been generated. Social institutions like the courts and the schools have been visibly affected. Moreover, the child abuse problem has been occupying center stage longer than many social issues do—30 years now in the case of physical abuse. Mobilization around dozens of other social problems—from lead poisoning to family abduction—have not been nearly so successful.

This success is explained by two factors. First, it has resulted from the coalition of two historically strong political and social forces giving momentum to the issue. Second, this coalition has been greatly facilitated by the fact that these problems tap into a very strong nexus of psychological and social concerns for which they have become a vehicle and a symbol.

First, underlying the social movement coalition, there has grown up in the last generation a large set of new occupational categories in our society with the function of ministering to families and children, directly and indirectly. These occupations now make up a large part of the personnel services sector of our economy—adding up to millions of jobs that didn't exist before. This sector includes many new professions in education, public health, medicine, law, and mental health. The issue of child abuse galvanizes these groups, because it clearly symbolizes and justifies their mission and is very consistent with their self-perceived role in society: to protect children by exercising professional expertise. As professionals they have had the time, the energy, and the skills to build and solidify this movement.

To this interest group has been added the weight and power of the women's movement, particularly in the area of concern about sexual abuse. Historically, political progress in child welfare has been linked to the success of feminism (Gordon, 1988), and the fact that women are disproportionate victims of sexual abuse has cemented this linkage in the modern period. Both feminists and child welfare professionals have been very successful in building social movements in the past (Rose, 1977). Both have become politically and socially influential, and both have achieved a great deal of moral authority. Their joining of forces around issues of child abuse has made them virtually irresistible.

But in addition to having a strong interest coalition, child abuse has also been a successful social issue because of the enormous symbolic strength it carries. We live in an era in which because of our relative prosperity, our ability to control fertility, and our medical advances over childhood mortality, we are increasingly psychologically invested in our children and their welfare. The child protection movement has been able to tap into the very evocative and sentimental imagery of protecting, rescuing, and comforting vulnerable children. No one who has seen the public service announcements for groups such as the National Committee for the Prevention of Child Abuse and Neglect can doubt the power of this.

But sexual abuse has been even more symbolically powerful than child abuse in general. The issue of sexual abuse has managed to unite three of the central preoccupations of the period and the generation. The first is sexuality and the new passion, after generations of silence and repression, to discuss and understand sexuality. The second preoccupation is with the relationship between the genders and the changing character of family. And the third preoccupation is with crime and justice. Anyone with any doubt about the historical centrality of these three themes should look at the current popular cinema: Its subject matter is primarily sex, crime, or changing gender and family relations. Sexual abuse conjoins these themes. It has fascinated people because, through learning about it and understanding it, they have obtained another vehicle to explore some of these preoccupying themes.

The Outlook for the Child Protection Movement

A strong social base and an evocative symbolic structure help to explain why child protection has been so successful as a social problem mobilization. But as sociological studies show, social problem mobilizations do not live forever, at least in the limelight (Hilgartner & Bosk, 1988). Sometimes they die, and sometimes they recede into the background. Coalitions splinter. Advocates become frustrated. The public and policy makers become bored.

Starting in the late 1980s, and extending into the early 1990s, we have seen growing signs of what has been called a "child abuse backlash" (Hechler, 1988). This backlash has included wide-ranging attacks in the media and by politicians on the field of child welfare advocacy and some of its leaders. A group of public figures has arisen who openly question some of the practices and assumptions in the field. Increasingly, newspaper stories have described instances of miscarriages of justice in child welfare practice (see Chapter 7). Some critics have begun to describe child abuse as a self-serving industry, child protection workers as zealots trampling the rights of innocent citizens, and courts as engaged in hysterical witch-hunts against innocent victims. Some of these attacks have appeared in relatively influential sources—such as the *Wall Street Journal*, CBS's *60 Minutes, Newsweek,* and the *Village Voice*. What does this portend? Is this the beginning of a decline for the child protection issue?

A first step to answering that question is to try to take stock of the strength and durability of the social and symbolic bases that underlie the child protection movement. Are there signs of erosion and weakening? Has the coalition lost its power or the symbols their grip?

For the most part, the social bases underpinning the child protection movement seem relatively strong, although not invulnerable. The women's movement has faced considerable backlash itself in recent years (Faludi, 1991), although it remains fairly potent. From the sociological point of view, the economic and political engines behind the women's movement—the increasing participation of women in the labor force and the political process—have not abated. True, in the late 1980s the feminist agenda turned from child abuse to other more central and increasingly threatened women's issues, such as abortion rights. But what is most crucial is the inexorable trend of women gaining access to positions of authority—in the professions and in government. The 1992 Democratic presidential victory certainly gave this trend a boost, and as women rise in authority, they should carry with them, as in the past (Gordon, 1988), a strong tilt toward issues of child welfare. This is a very major and long-term advantage for child protection advocacy.

At the same time, the other prong of the coalition, the child and family professions, is still growing. Some of their political agenda has been stymied, but will perhaps receive a boost under a Democratic administration. But irrespective of political conditions, one of the real assets of child protection advocacy is the huge number of professionals in related fields, such as medicine, law, and education, who have been trained and educated in child abuse concepts over the years and who have developed a certain confidence in them as a result of cumulative professional experience. These professionals have a relatively strong allegiance to these ideas that will resist erosion.

In addition, public support for child protection activities seems pretty strong. Public exposure to and knowledge about the problem of child abuse have been good and are getting better. For example, we have evidence in a recent study that 67% of U.S. children are receiving some sex abuse education in schools now, and that parents are highly approving of this trend (Finkelhor & Dzuiba-Leatherman, in press). Studies about the prevalence of child abuse in the general public suggest that there is a huge cadre of individuals with personal experience of the problem. Many of these individuals have been personally liberated by the media attention the problem has received. In surveys, they are among those most concerned about and supportive of action on this issue, and it seems likely that they will continue such support, if not publicly, at least within their informal social networks.

In summary, the social bases and support for the child protection movement itself appear strong at the present and for the near-term future.

Opposition Forces:
Interests and Countermovements

Social problem movements, even successful ones, face resistance, usually of two sorts: oppositional and inertial. The oppositional form consists of organized opposition groups—an example would be the Tobacco Institute, an organized group that has opposed the movement on behalf of nonsmoker's rights, or the National Rifle Association, which has opposed the gun control movement. The inertial resistance is just as real, but more diffuse: It consists of bureaucratic obstacles and delays, professional turf guarding, lack of funding, the pressure of other competing social problems advocates, and public apathy and boredom.

Within the oppositional form of resistance, a further distinction is worth making. This is between true organized opposing interests, on the one hand, and what have been termed *countermovements,* on the other. The Tobacco Institute is an example of an organized opposing interest (Troyer & Markle, 1983). From the beginning of nonsmoker's rights, the Tobacco Institute represented an interest opposed to that social movement. Similarly, the paper industry would be considered an opposing interest to the environmental movement for clean water.

In contrast, a countermovement is an opposition that develops *in response or in reaction* to the success of another social movement. It doesn't already exist, it develops later. Phyllis Schlafly and the Eagle Forum represent a countermovement, organized in response to the women's movement and the lobbying for the Equal Rights Amendment. What we are calling the child abuse *backlash* is also such a countermovement.

Countermovements are different in important ways from organized opposition groups. One crucial difference is that organized opposition groups are generally much stronger than countermovements. Organized opposition groups have historical and economic roots—such as those of the tobacco industry. They often have massive resources and a great deal of experience in public relations and political activism.

One of the somewhat unusual things about the mobilization around physical and sexual abuse as social problems is that *advocacy about these social problems grew with very little in the way of organized opposition.* Of course, the child protection movement had to deal with "inertial" resistance like bureaucratic foot-dragging and professional turf guarding. But no large, well-organized, entrenched interest group strongly and directly supported the abuse of children. The psychoanalytical wing of the psychiatric profession was initially skeptical about the existence of sexual abuse (Masson, 1984), but its opposition was trivial (and put up little in the way of a defense) compared to the concerted opposition forces that many if not most social problems movements face. Consider the opposition forces that confront advocates for other social problems: The movement for contraception and birth control, for example, must challenge the massive power of the Catholic church, and the movement to combat global warming faces the huge international industrial complex led by producers of fossil fuels. The movement to combat child abuse has certainly had to weather some opposition; the issue of sexual abuse in particular has roused doubts and fears—perhaps even some very deep psychological fears. But the opposition has been comparatively weakly organized. The child protection movement has been unusually fortunate in this way. But having had this generally free ride, the movement may be somewhat skittish, alarmist, and unseasoned when it comes to facing serious opposition.

Anatomy of the Backlash

To understand the child abuse backlash, it is important to understand the nature of countermovements in general. Some other examples of countermovement in recent times include the anti-ERA movement, the antibusing (for school integration) movement; and the current anti-gay rights movement. Sociologists have noted some characteristics of these countermovements (Mottl, 1980).

First, they are a reaction to the *success* of the movement they oppose. It is only when the initial movement gains real strength and begins to effect serious change that these countermovements crystalize.

Second, they are reactive and oppositional. They seldom have a program of their own; rather they stand against something.

Third, they tend to have a single-issue focus.

Fourth, they attack the means proposed by the initial movement rather than the ends. For example, they are not likely to contend that it is a bad idea to prevent child abuse (or achieve racial integration); rather they say that the advocates are going about it in the wrong way—being too zealous, too aggressive, and so forth. They focus on the means.

Fifth, they tend to mobilize predominantly from the ranks of the downwardly mobile, displaced, and déclassé segments of society.

Overall, in spite of the controversy they provoke, countermovements tend not to be all that successful for a number of reasons. Because they are late in getting organized, the initial movement usually has a big advantage over them. Being reactionary, they have a hard time inspiring people through idealism and visions of progress. Given their narrow focus, they have a hard time building coalitions. And finally, operating among the downwardly mobile, they tend to lack a powerful social base. In the end, they tend to act as irritants rather than true counterrevolutions. But under certain conditions they can achieve a lot of power and become a major obstacle for a social movement.

One such condition is when an initial social movement goes too far beyond a prevailing social consensus, or, in other words, seeks and achieves changes through influencing the elite without building a base of support in the public at large. This was partly the condition that produced successful countermovements against both school busing and abortion rights. The advocates for abortion rights and integration achieved dramatic changes from the top through the courts (*Brown v. Board of Education*, 1954, and *Roe v. Wade*, 1973), rather than through the grassroots, coalition-building, political process. So the changes came quickly without firm public support having been built. Both movements were vulnerable to a backlash. This can be the disadvantage of social change strategies that use the courts to bypass the slow process of politics.

A second condition that can lead to the success of a countermovement is when it is able to form a coalition with another stronger existing movement or institution. Thus the anti-ERA activists achieved success by joining forces with the preexisting Christian evangelical movement. This kind of alliance can happen when the counter-movement symbolizes some strong generalized value or concern that the larger institution already has as its goal. Frequently, the larger institution is already an organized political party or political interest group.

Now let us examine the backlash against the child protection movement to see if we can conjecture about what is likely to happen to it. First, and importantly, the backlash against the child protection movement has been relatively slow to mobilize. The social movement around physical child abuse dates from the early 1960s and is 30 years old; the movement around sexual abuse is close to 15 years old. The backlash—which only acquired an organizational framework in the late 1980s—is thus mobilizing late in the game.

The backlash also conforms to the propositions outlined earlier about countermovements. It can be described as a response to the success of the child protection movement—in particular, the large growth in the number of reports of abuse and state interventions in recent years. It is fairly oppositional and reactive; it has little in its agenda beside complaints about child welfare practices. And it is narrowly focused and seems to be attacking the means not the ends; backlash proponents don't object to ending child abuse, only over-zealousness on the part of child welfare authorities.

What is the social base for this backlash? Sociologically, it appears to consist of two main groups, with some peripheral and inconsistent allies. One main group is aggrieved parents who have been investigated for child abuse and believe they were unfairly treated or stigmatized in the process (Hechler, 1988; Spiegel, 1985). The social base of the backlash also includes some day care operators and teachers who had suspicions cast on them and feel their professional reputations have been compromised. Some are very angry and hurt—sometimes with good reason. These are the individuals who have provided the core energies behind groups like Victims of Child Abuse Laws (VOCAL) in various states and who have lobbied legislatures to pass laws to protect parents and restrain child protective agencies (see Chapter 4 for the VOCAL perspective).

The social base of the backlash also includes some parents who have been accused of abuse by their adult children and may have been sued or threatened with suits. These individuals have helped found organizations like the False Memory Syndrome (FMS) Foundation to help discredit adult children who claim to have recovered repressed memories of childhood abuse (*FMS Foundation Newsletter*, 1992). In addition, the aggrieved parents' group includes some parents—such as divorced fathers—who never actually suffered investigations or suspicions themselves, but having experienced devastating family conflicts, feel vulnerable to them.

The second main group involved in the backlash is attorneys. As child abuse reports have grown, so have prosecutions, and as allegations have touched even the middle class, more and more attorneys have in recent years found themselves representing people confronting child abuse allegations. As a result it has become a more specialized and defined field of practice. A network of experienced attorneys has assembled a body of literature, standard arguments and rationales on which to base a defense, and a group of experts and supporters who can be relied on to build these rationales (Coleman, 1986a, 1986b; Heeney, 1985; Howson, 1985). These rationales include the idea that child protection workers are generally overzealous in identifying abuse, that children can be easily manipulated to make or agree with false allegations, that a kind of witch-hunt mentality and child abuse hysteria blinds professionals, and so forth (Hechler, 1988). Attorneys have rightly recognized that to win child abuse defense cases it helps if their arguments have greater legitimacy among the public, among the judges, and among the professional community. So they have been active in making these arguments publicly and have provided financial support to other individuals active in the backlash.

In addition to these core groups, the backlash appears to have a few peripheral allies in the ranks of academics, professionals, legislators, and the media, but these allies may be inconsistent in their support and unrepresentative of the sentiments of their larger groups. For example, among academics, selected points of view from the backlash have gained support. Certain academics have criticized the way the social movement around child abuse has defined and stampeded the academic agenda. They have objected to premature judgments about the nature of children's sexual experiences (Okami, 1990) and premature consensus about the credibility of children's testimony. Among child welfare professionals, a few have dissented from the ideology around sexual abuse and some have perhaps opportunistically opted for financial gain and notoriety as opposition witnesses. Among politicians, some conservatives, in particular, who are concerned about budgets unbalanced by the expense of child welfare activities, have picked up some of the rhetoric of the backlash for arguing against government excess. Among the media, the backlash has drawn attention from journalists eager for a new angle on child abuse coverage.

The Prospects for the Backlash

Will this coalition of interests and ideas become powerful and influential? In evaluating the prospects for the backlash, a first question to ask relates to the vulnerability of the child protection movement itself. Earlier, I argued that one important condition for countermovement success was that an initial movement achieved changes by influencing an elite without building a base in the general public. However, this does not seem to apply (at least yet) to the case of child abuse. From the available evidence, there seems to be widespread public, professional, and political support for the current level of child abuse prevention, intervention, and even prosecution activities. Opinion polls suggest that the public wants more aggressive child protection activity, not less (Schulman, Ronca, and Bucuvalas, Inc., 1988). The public is more concerned about abusers who go free than about people who are unfairly prosecuted, more worried about damage to child witnesses than protection of defendants' rights. When asked to evaluate a specific backlash proposal— limiting child protection investigations to cases of demonstrable injury and harm as opposed to aggressively investigating all abuse reports—the public strongly favored aggressive investigating.

These polls, although a bit dated, do show fairly clear public support behind the activities of the child protection movement. In contrast to the early abortion and school-busing successes using the courts, progress on child abuse has occurred slowly and incrementally and in a relatively decentralized fashion through a process of public education and community organization. It has not been imposed from above and run ahead of social consensus. Such consensus could fracture quickly if, for example, child advocates suddenly passed laws outlawing corporal punishment by parents (as Sweden and some other Northern European countries have done). But even though such measures have been proposed and have some support among child advocates, their implementation is far from imminent.

In assessing the prospects for the backlash, a second question concerns its social base and whether it is likely to expand rapidly. The backlash attorneys are not a strong social base by themselves. Hired attorneys influence legislation, but they do not make social movements on their own. Moreover, defending against child abuse charges is not a legal subspecialty that will ever offer huge financial or status rewards. The number of lawyers involved and their influence and power are likely to remain small.

So, the aggrieved parents are the important core of the backlash movement if it is to grow. In some ways they do have a potentially evocative issue that could possibly resonate with a broader base in the public at large. Parents in the United States today do feel insecure. They lack confidence in their authority and in themselves as parents. They are bombarded by advice and criticism from experts and professionals. They feel they have increasingly little influence over their children as schools, television, advertising, and so forth extend their grasp. The risks of divorce and family breakdown hound them constantly. When they get caught up in the throes of divorce, as many do, it can be personally devastating. There is a lot of dry tinder here waiting for a possible explosion, and parents could be galvanized into a hunt for scapegoats. Two obvious targets are the state and the professionals—child protective services and child experts.

Although this scenario could potentially happen, it is not happening right now. Right now, in fact, parents on the whole have a lot of respect for the experts. Most have felt helped and assisted in their parenting through the advice they've received from magazines, television, and books. Most parents also do not feel threatened in their parenting by the state; there just aren't that many investigations occurring. The generalized malaise parents feel is more directed against the media, against drugs, and against the youth culture. Aggrieved parents who have been wronged by the child welfare system have an uphill battle to become the spokespeople of parental alienation in this country.

What about the peripheral allies? Is there an opening here for alliances that could catapult aggrieved parents into a more powerful coalition? Possibly, but it seems unlikely. The academic allies tend to be just what one finds everywhere in academia—iconoclasts, freethinkers, people who want to ask hard and unpopular questions. They do not really build movements in the absence of other strong social bases. In any case, most of these iconoclasts would feel grave discomfort in any serious ideological alliance with the popular backlash advocates.

The potential for a backlash alliance with the professional community also seems dim. Only when you have a large group of skeptical professionals—such as the large number of scientists publicly doubtful about the greenhouse effect—do you have the possibility for a strong countermovement alliance. There are some such skeptical professionals in child welfare, but they are a small group. And their skepticism is not about fundamental questions, but rather about tactical issues—for example, not about whether child abuse prevention education is an attack on family autonomy, but rather whether it should be taught to preschoolers, or to parents rather than children themselves.

There may be some budding politicians who will try in the future to build careers battling the so-called child abuse industry. But it is a risky course for a politician right now to seem opposed to fighting child abuse. The child protection movement has been surprisingly effective in sustaining bipartisan political support for its activities. It is true that the issue of limiting state intervention in family life fits into the conservative agenda. But conservatives have also been drawn to support of the child abuse issue because it fits their anticrime agenda.

Finally, some of the biggest successes of the backlash to date have been in the form of the influential and sometimes sympathetic media editorializing it has received. Dozens of articles critical of the child protection movement arose out of the McMartin preschool case and other day care cases (Hentoff, 1992a; Rabinowitz, 1990). The failed prosecution in Jordan, Minnesota, spawned similar stories and editorials. Some newspapers, such as the *San Diego Union*, have mobilized relentless unfavorable coverage of local child abuse authorities. Might the media turn against child abuse and spurn it as effectively as it once embraced it?

First, in spite of perceptions, the media rarely create social movements or countermovements on their own. It takes organizations and ideologies to build movements. The media cover and respond to these organizations and activities, and because the public first notices movements through the media, we often think of them as media inspired. But movements need some strong organization outside the media.

A movement without a strong base can only be sustained by media attention for a short time. It is interesting to note that in spite of the barrage of critical articles and the ultimate failure of the McMartin prosecution, the backlash did not mushroom as a result, as many people had feared. This was probably because there was little formal countermovement organization to sustain it.

Summarizing the argument in terms of social forces, as a social movement, the child protection coalition seems to be holding on to its hegemony, whereas the backlash appears rather marginal in comparison. This is not to say that the backlash has not had its impact. Many individuals in the child protection field can testify to the intense personal and professional consequences that conflicts with the backlash have had.

But it may also be true that child advocates have a low tolerance for political conflict, having had a relatively opposition-free ascent to policy prominence. This sensitivity may be compounded by the character of the people who are drawn to the field. Many people who go into child welfare work do so to be healers, not warriors. They also identify with *victims*. Many people with such an orientation tend to be alarmed by conflict or the possibility of becoming victims themselves. This may result in an exaggerated perception of the power of the backlash compared to their own. The reality is that other social problems movements have grown and prospered even in the face of much more powerful opposition than the child abuse backlash has mounted. In fact, opposition can be a tonic for a social movement. It can keep it from becoming complacent and arrogant. The child protection movement does not appear to be in imminent peril.

Future Developments

On the basis of this analysis, what is likely to happen? The child protection movement is still in a position of great strength and is able to set much of the agenda. The fate of the backlash may well depend on how the child protection movement responds. The movement can fuel the backlash either by giving it additional fodder to exploit or through open and bitter conflict that raises its visibility. If the movement steers some middle course, though, correcting problems that make it vulnerable to criticism, but not focusing exclusively on the backlash, the backlash may well recede or be coopted.

A central strategy for the child protection movement should be to have balanced and primarily proactive goals: (a) to maintain its strong ties to and expand its powerful social base; (b) to remain dynamic, creative, and flexible as a social movement; and, last, (c) to worry about guarding its flanks against the development of a countermovement linked to other broad social or political forces.

Although the ties of the child protection movement to its social base—child-oriented professionals, adult survivors of child abuse, and the women's movement—are very strong, they can be reinforced and renewed. One of the biggest dangers is splintering and division within this coalition. The most likely cleavage line is the one between professionals and nonprofessionals, but this coalition probably will not splinter if it is tended adequately.

The child protection movement actually has many obvious opportunities to even expand its social base. For example, the general criminal justice community has in recent years become more interested in child abuse. Ties with criminologists, judges, and other criminal justice personnel may get stronger. There are other opportunities for social problems coalitions to develop as well. For example, because it is increasingly clear that a childhood history of sexual abuse is a risk factor for unprotected sexual behavior, the AIDS movement may become more involved in child abuse prevention and detection. As a result of concern over cocaine-addicted babies and the children of drug-addicted parents, common interests between preventing child abuse and drug abuse may develop. These are areas where the child protection movement may be strengthened by ties to other interest coalitions.

The addition of these new issues and coalitions may also forestall the danger of "social problem fatigue." Every social problem movement eventually comes up against the fact that the public and even concerned professionals tire of hearing about it (Downs, 1972). However, new angles give the problem some freshness and dynamism. The public and professionals get particularly tired of problems that seem hopeless and intractable. One of the reasons why child abuse may be a more active public issue today than the problem of poverty, for example, is that people think it's easier to make progress against child abuse. The child protection movement needs to avoid the Chicken Little syndrome and publicize its successes.

Another element that may influence the strength of the child protection movement is the quality of its research base. In today's social policy environment, research is a valuable currency in the market of social problem advocacy. It is also a currency that is very difficult for a countermovement to match. Already, child advocates have had some success checking some of the more damaging claims of the backlash through research: For example, the idea that non-abused children can be easily induced to make false allegations of abuse (Goodman & Clarke-Stewart, 1991).

It is important that child advocates respond to, and not simply ignore, the backlash. It is now an axiom of public relations that one should never allow oneself to be "Dukakis'd," that is, to let damaging charges stand without a rebuttal. To some extent, the fate of the backlash depends on there being credible counterarguments to the backlash.

Social problem movement advocates frequently make a mistake in thinking that they have to convince the opposition. It is not the opposition that needs convincing: The appropriate audience is the people who might potentially be enfolded into a countermovement coalition—for example, the politicians, the media, the academics, and particularly, the beleaguered and dispirited parents. This situation affects the kind of rebuttal that is called for.

Ultimately, what may most determine the fate of the backlash is not simply rebuttal, but how the child welfare movement responds to what is valid and plausible in the backlash critique. If child advocates improve the quality of investigations, provide more rights for parents reported for abuse, and make other changes, they may deprive the backlash of much of its agenda. Such self-scrutiny and reform should be relatively easy for a movement in as secure a position as the child protection movement is today.

TWO

Definition and Origins of the Backlash Against Child Protection

JOHN E. B. MYERS

There is growing evidence of a backlash against child protection. A backlash is a strong adverse reaction to a political or social movement (*Webster's Ninth New Collegiate Dictionary*, 1985). In common parlance, a backlash is a negative response to a constructive or positive step forward. For our purposes, the positive step forward is the progress during the past two decades on behalf of abused children, and the backlash is the escalating chorus of criticism directed against professionals working to protect children.

In defining the backlash, it is important to distinguish legitimate criticism from illegitimate criticism of the child protection system. Although it is sometimes difficult to distinguish the two, it is important to draw the line. Failure to recognize the difference between legitimate and illegitimate criticism obscures the fact that criticism is not inevitably negative in effect. Far from it. Criticism plays an important role in exposing incompetence and improving complex bureaucracies. Nevertheless, even legitimate criticism can be harmful. There can be too much of a "good thing." The cumulative effect of the current wave of criticism is likely to be greater than the sum of its parts, undermining society's commitment to child protection.

When does criticism cross the line from legitimate to illegitimate? Illegitimate criticism distorts or seriously exaggerates the faults of the child protection system. Within the realm of illegitimate criticism, it is useful to draw a further distinction: between misguided but honest criticism, on the one hand, and what may be called malignant criticism, on the other. The motives of the misguided but honest critic differ markedly from those of the malignant critic. Professionals should reach out to misguided but well-intended critics. By contrast, when a backlash critic's motives are malignant, the response should be different in kind and purpose. (Illegitimate criticism is further described in Chapter 7.)

Child Protection Has Always Been Criticized

Most professionals working with abused and neglected children are concerned about the backlash. To place this concern in perspective, it is worth remembering that criticism of child protection is anything but new. Criticism waxes and wanes, but never abates completely. The symptoms of the backlash "subside and resurface periodically" (Faludi, 1991, p. xix).

From the dawn of organized child protection in the 1850s, there has been a bumper crop of criticism. By the middle of the 19th century, Eastern cities were growing rapidly, swelled by waves of immigration. The industrial revolution was steaming ahead, fueled by an army of poorly paid workers, including thousands of children. As cities expanded, increasing numbers of children fell into necessitous circumstances. The most outspoken mid-century critic of conditions facing city children was Charles Loring Brace. In 1852, Brace graduated from Union Theological Seminary and began working with the poor in New York's sweltering slums. Brace was particularly taken aback by the plight of the children. With help from interested clergy, Brace founded the New York Children's Aid Society in 1853 and served as its secretary until his death in 1890 (Bremner, 1970; Leiby, 1978; Tiffin, 1982).

Brace's solution for children trapped in urban squalor was to wrench them away from their poverty-stricken parents and send them "out west" to grow up as foster children in rural Midwestern states. During Brace's administration, the New York Children's Aid Society placed more than 90,000 children (Leiby, 1978; Radbill, 1987). Not surprising, Brace came in for considerable criticism, particularly from Catholics, who believed that Brace's hidden agenda was converting poor Catholic children to Protestantism by placing them in Protestant foster homes. Brace was also criticized for lax supervision of his far-flung foster children.

The Massachusetts Society for the Prevention of Cruelty to Children (MSPCC) provides another illustration of early criticism. The MSPCC was one of the most influential private child protection societies in the early years of the 20th century (Gordon, 1988). In Boston, "the Cruelty" was used to describe the work of the MSPCC. But it was not the term used by social workers to describe abuse and neglect of children. Oh no. "The Cruelty" was coined by poor people in Boston's slums to describe the social workers from the protection society! One tenement resident with a grudge against another would yell across the back fence, "You'd better not cross me or I'll call the Cruelty and they'll take your kids away."

Thus child protection has always been criticized. Indeed, criticism is inevitable. Intervention in the family offends entrenched U.S. traditions. Intervention violates the sanctity of the family. Intervention threatens male dominance in family matters. Finally, intervention is inherently coercive and confrontational.

Although efforts to prevent child abuse and neglect have always been criticized, the fundamental mission of the child protection movement is morally defensible and so important that efforts to protect children have continually weathered the storm and moved forward. Today, the question is how well child protection will weather the current maelstrom of criticism.

Sources of the Backlash

Although the backlash focuses on all types of maltreatment, child sexual abuse garners more attention from critics than other types of abuse and neglect. Why is the backlash particularly venomous regarding child sexual abuse? There are three primary reasons: (a) the degree of emotion generated by sexual abuse of children, (b) society's blind spot for sexual abuse, and (c) the failings of the child protection system.

Emotions Run High

The emotionality associated with child sexual abuse fuels polarization and backlash. To appreciate why child sexual abuse evokes such strong emotion in adults, it is helpful to engage in a simple mental exercise. First, put any thought of child abuse completely out of mind. Shift your thoughts entirely away from child abuse. This done, ask the following question: What do adults feel strongly about? Children come immediately to mind. Normal, healthy, non-abused children evoke strong emotions in adults.

Now put children to one side and ask the same question: What else do adults feel strongly about? Victimization. Few subjects evoke stronger emotions than victimization. Most of us are victims at some point, and the anger and helplessness that accompany victimization are strong emotions indeed.

Finally, put children and victimization aside, and ask once more: What do adults feel strongly about? Sex! Few subjects evoke stronger or more varied emotions than sex and sexuality.

Now, put the three together—children, victimization, and sex—to form child sexual abuse, and the stage is set for emotional fireworks. Few events evoke stronger feelings of outrage, scandal, and pity than the sexual victimization of helpless children. Thus one element of the backlash is the sheer strength of emotion the subject stirs up in adults.

Society's Blind Spot

Sexual abuse of children is as old as humankind. In *The History of Childhood*, de Mause (1974) writes that the further back in history one goes, the more likely children are to be sexually abused. Yet society is extremely reluctant to acknowledge the reality of child sexual abuse. Summit (1988) writes:

> In every eye there is a spot that is incapable of sight. . . . Throughout history there have been human beliefs and group phenomena that exhibit the perceptual equivalent of a blind spot. A people will develop a cherished view and defend it against revision, despite the presence of a glaring central defect. It took 18 centuries to give up the sacred notion that the world was the center of the universe, for example, despite an irrefutable accumulation of evidence to the contrary.
>
> Something of the same dilemma confronts the potential believer in child sexual abuse. Anyone proclaiming it as vitally important imposes a dismal flaw in our hope for a just and fair society. All of our systems of justice, reason, and power have been adjusted to ignore the possibility of such a fatal flaw. Our very sense of enlightenment

insists that anything *that* important could not escape our attention. Where could it hide? Parents would find it out. Doctors would see it. The courts would spot it. Victims would tell their psychiatrists. It would be obvious in psychological tests. Our best minds would know it. It is more reasonable to argue that young upstarts are making trouble. You can't trust kids. Untrained experts are creating a wave of hysteria. They ask leading questions. No family is safe from the invasion of the childsavers. (p. 51)

The reality of child sexual abuse "has repeatedly surfaced into public and professional awareness in the past century and a half, only to be resuppressed by the negative reaction it elicits" (Olafson, Corwin, & Summit, 1993, p. 8). The first modern acknowledgment of child sexual abuse occurred in 19th-century France. In 1857, the respected French physician Ambrose Tardieu published a book describing thousands of cases of child sexual abuse. Tardieu and others sparked short-lived interest in the study of child sexual abuse. Summit (1988) describes the backlash that awaited Tardieu and like-minded professionals:

Tardieu generated an oasis of concern for children in a generally indifferent, adult-preoccupied society. Challenging the tradition that children typically lied about sexual assault, a few clinicians dared to argue for the truth and reality of those complaints. Such trust in children invited adult retaliation. Despite Tardieu's enormous influence on other aspects of forensic medicine, his belief in sexual abuse was rejected by his successors. (p. 46)

In 1880, scarcely a year after Tardieu's death, a speaker at the French Academy of Medicine gave a speech titled "Simulation of Sexual Attacks on Young Children," in which the speaker warned that respectable men are targeted for blackmail by depraved children and their lower class parents. Another successor to Tardieu, Paul Brouardel, remarked, "Girls accuse their fathers of imaginary assaults on them or on other children in order to obtain their freedom to give themselves over to debauchery" (Summit, 1988, p. 46). Brouardel asserted that 60% to 80% of children's complaints were fabricated. Thus Tardieu's efforts to acknowledge the reality of child sexual abuse were quickly snuffed out in a forceful backlash.

The second acknowledgment of child sexual abuse occurred in 1896, and Sigmund Freud himself brought the issue to the fore. In

April of that year Freud presented his paper "The Aetiology of Hysteria," in which he argued that the neurotic symptoms he observed in his adult patients were caused by sexual abuse during childhood. Freud called this explanation for neurosis the seduction theory. The theory received a decidedly cool reception from the Vienna Society for Psychiatry and Neurology, and within a short time Freud wrote, "I am as isolated as you could wish me to be: the word has been given out to abandon me, and a void is forming around me" (Masson, 1984, p. 10).

Freud abandoned the seduction theory and replaced it with the Oedipus complex. Summit (1988) observes that "the Oedipus Complex, which was to become the irreducible foundation of psychoanalysis, was a perfect reversal of the seduction theory. Now children were traumatized not by actual sexual assault but by projections of their own wishful masturbatory fantasies" (p. 48). Thus Freud bowed to criticism of his original belief in the reality of child sexual abuse, and as he did so, the sun set on the second acknowledgment of child sexual abuse.

Freud's impact on society was immense, and was felt in many quarters, including law. Under Freud's influence, the brilliant legal scholar John Henry Wigmore was persuaded that, in sex offense cases, women and girls were not to be trusted. In his monumental treatise on evidence, first published in 1904, Wigmore wrote:

> Modern psychiatrists have amply studied the behavior of errant young girls and women coming before the courts in all sorts of cases. Their psychic complexes are multifarious, distorted partly by inherent defects, partly by diseased derangements or abnormal instincts, partly by bad social environment, partly by temporary physiological or emotional conditions. One form taken by these complexes is that of contriving false charges of sexual offenses by men. The unchaste (let us call it) mentality finds incidental but direct expression in the narration of imaginary sex incidents of which the narrator is the heroine or the victim. On the surface the narration is straightforward and convincing. The real victim, however, too often in such cases is the innocent man; for the respect and sympathy naturally felt by any tribunal for a wronged female helps to give easy credit to such a plausible tale. . . . *No judge should ever let a sex offense charged go to the jury unless the female complainant's social history and mental makeup have been examined and testified to by a qualified physician.* (1904/1970, pp. 736-737)

Like Freud, Wigmore was extremely influential. Wigmore's treatise carried such weight that many courts adopted his suspicions about women and girls in sex offense cases (Myers, 1992a).

Despite the influence of men like Freud and Wigmore, child protection professionals long appreciated the reality of child sexual abuse. The early records of the Massachusetts Society for the Prevention of Cruelty to Children (MSPCC) reveal that incest made up approximately 10% of the caseload. Although sexual abuse figured prominently in the work of early child protection societies, the general public did not hear about it. The MSPCC, for example, recognized that sexual abuse was common, but considered it too revolting to publish (Gordon, 1988).

Because society has a blind spot for child sexual abuse, the problem is periodically pushed below the surface of recognition, where it is ignored. The apparent "discovery" of child sexual abuse in the late 1970s was nothing more than the latest in a series of *re*discoveries. The critical issue today is whether society will once again shut its eyes.

The Shortcomings of Child Protection

Much of the backlash is attributable to the shortcomings of the child protection system. In 1990 the U.S. Advisory Board on Child Abuse and Neglect warned that the child protection system is in crisis, and that fundamental problems permeate the system (1990). In particular, the board pointed to "the overload of cases; the crisis in foster care; and the absence of a focus on the needs of children" (p. 34).

Although many of child protection's shortcomings are beyond the control of professionals working in the system, the professional community shares the blame for a significant portion of the backlash. Indeed, it is no exaggeration to say that at least 50% of the backlash is a self-inflicted wound. Four specific failings of the professional community are outlined below. Each contributes to the backlash.

A. *Exaggerated Statements That Contribute to the Backlash*

People who feel strongly about issues sometimes slip into hyperbole. Few professionals feel more strongly about their work than the social workers, mental health professionals, doctors, prosecutors, and others who devote their professional lives to protecting and treating children. Given their zeal on behalf of children, it comes as no surprise that an occasional professional exaggerates. If the professional happens to be a leader in the field, the exaggeration may be adopted by other professionals, and in rare cases, may take on a life of its own.

The cardinal illustration of exaggeration that has come back to haunt child protection is the oft-repeated, "Children do not lie about sexual abuse." To place this statement in context, recall that throughout much of the 20th century, psychologists urged us not to believe children (Goodman, 1984). "Children are too suggestible," psychologists warned. "Children live in a fantasy world and cannot differentiate real from imaginary," they cautioned. In 1926, a psychologist wrote, "Create if you will, an idea of what the child is to hear or see, and the child is very likely to hear or see what you desire" (Brown, 1926, p. 133). Fortunately, modern psychology is exploding the old bromide that children have poor memories, are invariably suggestible, and cannot distinguish real from pretend (Au, 1992; Goodman & Bottoms, 1993). Yet, in recent years, some professionals went too far to redress the inaccurate historical picture of children's capabilities, making indefensible statements such as "We know children do not lie about sexual abuse," and "We must believe the children." Writing in 1988, Mantell observed that "an article of faith seems to have arisen which holds that 'children never lie about something like this' " (p. 618; Everson, Boat, Bourg, & Robertson, in press).

All people who have children of their own, or who understand children, know that children lie. Many normal, happy 4-year-olds lie like a thief when caught red-handed in the cookie jar. Children do lie. In the context of sexual abuse, however, clinical experience and empirical research teach us that children usually tell the truth as they understand it (Jones & McGraw, 1987). Yet an occasional child deliberately fabricates an allegation (Bussey, Lee, & Grimbeek, 1993). The important point is not that fabrication *never* occurs, but that it is *uncommon*. Thus it is simply false to say that "children do not lie about sexual abuse." The discerning listener quickly exposes this statement for what it is—indefensible exaggeration. The statement, and statements like it, invite criticism. More important, such statements raise doubts not only about the motives of the speaker, but through guilt by association, the competence of the entire child protection community.

B. Failing to Learn From the Critics

Too often, professionals do not listen carefully or give credit where due to the critics of child protection. One of the most vociferous critics is the organization called Victims of Child Abuse Laws (VOCAL). Unfortunately, VOCAL's rhetoric sometimes crosses the line into irresponsible backlash because it so far exaggerates the faults of the child protection system that it materially undermines society's willingness to protect children. Many of VOCAL's proposed reforms would actually harm children. In the name of "family rights," VOCAL would throw the baby out with the bath water. Yet there is more than a kernel of truth in many of VOCAL's criticisms. That is why VOCAL has a chapter in this book. (See Chapter 4 for VOCAL's perspective.) Unless professionals listen to what VOCAL has to say, it will be difficult for them to respond effectively to the many inaccuracies in VOCAL's writing, lobbying, and advocacy. Of equal importance, when professionals close their ears, they fail to appreciate *valid* criticism that could improve the child protection system. Finally, refusal to consider the views of "outsiders" is the hallmark of high-handed, haughty bureaucrats. An attitude of condescension is inevitably followed by the inefficiency so common in entrenched bureaucracy. Child protection professionals should build bridges to critics rather than circle the wagons to exclude ideas that originate in criticism.

C. Letting Advocacy Get Ahead of Knowledge

In their enthusiasm to protect children, professionals occasionally exceed the bounds of current knowledge. Although such forays into speculation usually arise from benign motives, venturing beyond the limits of defensible knowledge contributes to the backlash. Justice Brandeis of the U.S. Supreme Court warned long ago of the danger in well-intended but misguided zealotry, writing that "experience should teach us most to be on our guard to protect liberty when the government's purposes are beneficent. . . . The greatest dangers to liberty lurk in insidious encroachments by men of zeal, well-meaning but without understanding" (*Olmstead v. United States*, 1928, p. 479). Three examples illustrate the danger of exceeding current knowledge.

Expert testimony that is carefully limited to the bounds of current knowledge plays a useful role in some child sexual abuse cases.

Unfortunately, during the 1980s, and to a lesser extent today, a few prosecutors offered "expert" testimony that exceeded proper limits. In a 1984 case, for example, a psychiatrist testified that there "was no doubt whatsoever" that a child was an incest victim (*State v. Haseltine*, 1984). It should have been obvious in 1984 that the expert was far too unequivocal in his opinion. Indeed, such certainty is unwarranted a decade later.

Judges react with understandable impatience to "expert" testimony that exceeds the limits of current knowledge. Such testimony adds nothing to the search for truth and prejudices the defendant's right to a fair trial. Persistent use of sloppy expert testimony can lead to the kind of judicial backlash that occurred in Pennsylvania in 1992. In a decision called *Commonwealth v. Dunkle* (1992), the Pennsylvania Supreme Court essentially outlawed *any* use in child sexual abuse prosecutions of expert testimony from mental health professionals. Who bears the responsibility for this unfortunate decision? The blame lies less with the Pennsylvania Supreme Court than with the prosecutors who offered, and the mental health professionals who provided, the poorly informed expert testimony that eventually led the court to throw up its hands in frustration and conclude that mental health professionals have nothing of value to contribute.

A second example of advocacy that exceeds the limits of knowledge concerns the way children are interviewed about suspected sexual abuse. Poor interviewing, particularly excessive use of leading questions, contributes significantly to skepticism about professional competence and children's credibility. Prior to 1990, the way children were interviewed was seldom mentioned in court decisions. Today, however, defense attorneys frequently concentrate their attack on the interviewer. Beginning with the U.S. Supreme Court's 1990 decision in *Idaho v. Wright*, an increasing number of appellate court decisions focus on investigative interviews (e.g., *Felix v. State*, 1993). In late 1993, for example, the highly publicized conviction of day care teacher Kelly Michaels was reversed in part because of the way the preschool-age children were interviewed (*State v. Michaels*, 1993). An excerpt from one interview supports the conclusion that the conviction could not stand. The child was interviewed by a social worker and a police officer:

> **Worker:**   Don't be so unfriendly. I thought we were buddies last time.

Child: Nope, not any more.

Worker: We have gotten a lot of other kids to help us since I last saw you. . . . Did we tell you that Kelly is in jail?

Child: Yes. My mother already told me.

Worker: Did I tell you that this is the guy (pointing to police officer) that arrested her? . . . Well, we can get out of here real quick if you just tell me what you told me that last time, when we met.

Child: I forgot.

Worker: No you didn't. I know you didn't.

Child: I did! I did!

Worker: I thought we were friends last time.

Child: I'm not your friend any more!

Worker: How come?

Child: I hate you!

Worker: You have no reason to hate me. We were buddies when you left.

Child: I hate you now!

Worker: Oh, you do not, you secretly like me, I can tell.

Child: I hate you.

Worker: Oh, come on. We talked to a few more of your buddies. And everyone told me about the nap room, and the bathroom stuff, and the music room stuff, and the choir stuff, and the peanut butter stuff, and everything. . . . All your buddies [talked]. . . . Come on, do you want to help us out? Do you want to keep her in jail? I'll let you hear your voice and play with the tape recorder; I need your help again. Come on. . . . Real quick, will you just tell me what happened with the wooden spoon? Let's go.

Child: I forgot.

Police: Now listen, you have to behave.

Worker: Do you want me to tell [the boy] to behave? Are you going to be a good boy, huh? While you are here, did he [the police officer] show you his badge and his handcuffs? . . . Back to what happened to you with the wooden spoon. If you don't remember words, maybe you can show me [with anatomical dolls].

Child: I forgot what happened, too.

Worker: You remember. You told your mommy about everything about the music room and the nap room, and all that stuff. You want to help her stay in jail, don't you?

> So she doesn't bother you any more and so she doesn't
> tell you any more scary stories. (quoted in Ceci &
> Bruck, 1993, p. 423)

Although there is no one "correct" way to interview children, there is a sizeable literature on interviewing and a consensus about what *not* to do. Professionals who persist in using indefensible interview techniques wreak havoc in individual cases and fuel the backlash.

As a final example of advocacy that gets ahead of knowledge, consider the explosive issue of ritualistic and satanic abuse of children. As this book goes to press in 1994, there is little consensus on the meaning of "ritual" or "satanic" abuse, let alone on the scope of the phenomenon. Although few would deny the occasional occurrence of sexual abuse with ritualistic overtones, some professionals and adult survivors believe that ritualistic and satanic abuse are widespread. Some postulate a nationwide satanic conspiracy. On the other hand, there are knowledgeable professionals who are very skeptical of such claims (Lanning, 1992).

Where does the truth lie regarding ritualistic and satanic abuse? Examination of this perplexing and frightening subject leads to but one conclusion: At this time it is impossible to reach any firm conclusions about widespread ritual or satanic abuse of children. In light of current knowledge, the most rational position is to keep an open mind, tempered with healthy skepticism, about the plausibility of such claims. One thing that is clear, however, is that the burden of proof lies squarely on the shoulders of those asserting widespread ritualistic and satanic abuse. Until this burden is satisfied with convincing evidence, child protection professionals would do well to avoid public statements that can be interpreted as supporting the existence of such abuse. Careless statements on this subject invite not only criticism but ridicule (Curtiss, 1992; Wright, 1993). Ultimately, such ridicule could spread, insidiously undermining public willingness to respond to more "mundane" forms of child sexual abuse.

D. CPS Is the Most Important Link
in the Child Protection Chain

County child protective services (CPS) agencies are the most important link in the child protection chain. The other links are medicine, nursing, law, mental health, judiciary, probation, police, and related professions. Although CPS is the most important link in the chain, few would deny that it is the weakest (Hechler, 1988). But why? The weakness of CPS has nothing to do with the dedication, intelligence, and caring of CPS social workers, most of whom perform well under extraordinarily trying circumstances. Indeed, compared to the day-to-day responsibilities of CPS social workers, the responsibilities of doctors, lawyers, judges, and mental health professionals are child's play.

The weakness of CPS results from several factors. First, social work is accorded lower professional status in society than law, medicine, or psychology. Not only is social work lower on the status totem pole, social work itself is hierarchically divided, with clinical practice higher in prestige than public administration. The low social status of social work undermines the fabric of the profession. For example, although CPS social workers are expected to exercise the wisdom of Solomon, their income hardly compares to Solomon's riches or, for that matter, to the income of many doctors, lawyers, and psychologists. It is sadly ironic that the profession with the most complex and demanding responsibilities receives the lowest professional status and remuneration.

Probably the major contributor to weakness in CPS is chronically inadequate funding. Although CPS is given Herculean responsibilities, it has *always* lacked the resources to do the job. As long ago as 1968, Vincent DeFrancis described a nationwide study of child protective services and lamented that "most disturbing was the finding that no state and no community has developed a Child Protective Service program adequate in size to meet the service needs of all reported cases of child neglect, abuse and exploitation" (1968, p. 25). In 1949, juvenile court judges echoed a similar refrain, writing that "our juvenile courts are not well equipped with probation, psychiatric, and other essential services, except in certain large centers, and even there they fall far short of the desirable" (Council of Juvenile Court Judges, 1949, p. 20). Thus, even in the "good old days," before the modern crush of cases, CPS was underfunded. By 1976 reports of child abuse and neglect had risen to 416,000 a year, and by 1992 the number had soared to a staggering 2.9 million! Overall, child maltreatment reports have maintained steady growth, increasing an average of 6% annually since 1985. Yet, in most communities, funding for CPS continues to lose ground.

Professionals in the trenches of child protection may be tempted to argue that inadequate funding is not their responsibility. Worrying about budgets is a headache for "higher ups." Although there is an element of truth in this defense, adequate funding will be forthcoming only when everyone in child protection labors at the same oar. All professionals must contribute to the fight for dollars.

Conclusion

An effective response to the backlash requires insight into the nature of the beast. In particular, it is important to understand the origins and cyclical nature of the backlash. Society's recognition of child abuse as a widespread problem is tenuous, half-hearted, and grudging, and professionals must be alert for rumblings of disbelief. Today, such rumblings are heard across the United States and in Europe. With society predisposed to ignore the uncomfortable reality of child abuse, the escalating backlash places us on the brink of a new era of disbelief.

THREE

The Backlash From the Perspective of a County Child Protective Services Administrator

SYLVIA PIZZINI

Background: The Child Protective Services Challenge

Every state has enacted public policies in accordance with federal law for the protection of abused children, rehabilitation of abusive parents, and provision of adoptive or foster homes for children who cannot live safely in their own home. In California, for example, the program is officially known as "Child Welfare Services" and is defined as follows:

Public social services which are directed towards the accomplishment of any or all the following purposes: protecting and promoting the welfare of all children, including handicapped, homeless, dependent, or neglected children; preventing or remedying, or assisting in the solution of problems which may result in, the neglect, abuse, exploitation, or delinquency of children; preventing the unnecessary separation of children from their families by identifying family problems, assisting families in resolving their problems, and preventing the breakup of the family where the prevention of child removal is desirable and possible; restoring to their families children who have ·been removed, by the provision of services to the children and the

families; identifying children to be placed in suitable adoptive homes,
in cases where restoration to the biological family is not possible or
appropriate; and assuring adequate care of children away from their
homes, in cases where the child cannot be returned home or cannot
be placed for adoption. (California Welfare and Institutions Code,
1993, Section 16501)

This general policy statement and statements like it in other states
have generated a multitude of supporting statutory, regulatory, and
case law mandates for implementation by local child protective
services (CPS) agencies. An important assumption underlying broad
statements of policy is that federal, state, and local governments
have a role in ensuring that children are provided safe homes and
that parents are able to care for and support their children. In
defining specifically what government's role should be, it is necessary to consider our social values, professional social work standards, the preferences of the general public, and the dictates of court
and statutory laws. Needless to say, this process presents complex
and evolving challenges.

In this chapter, I first describe the landmark national policy enact-
ments related to abuse and neglect of children. I then look at value
conflicts and inconsistencies inherent in the national policy framework. These conflicts and inconsistencies feed into the backlash
against CPS. I go on to examine the structures within CPS that are
designed to provide checks and balances in decision making and
discuss interorganizational collaboration intended to promote openness of decision making. The checks and balances built into the CPS
system, along with procedures to increase interorganizational cooperation, undermine many of the claims made by the backlash. Likewise, a review of services provided by CPS agencies over the last
decade shows progress that belies the allegations of backlash pro-
moters. I conclude with a discussion of how I view the backlash after
spending more than 25 years as a social worker and administrator
of CPS in California.

Landmarks in National Policy
Regarding Child Abuse and Neglect

Most citizens agree that there should be laws that allow government to intrude into the privacy of the family when children are

suffering maltreatment. There is debate, however, about what the criteria for intervention should be. For the first century and a half of the nation's existence, the United States did not have a uniform national child welfare policy. State and local governments, religious groups, and private charities provided services based on their conclusions regarding how to reach out to abused and neglected children and their parents.

A unified national policy did not come easily. There were several unsuccessful attempts to pass federal legislation. It took a national crisis, the Great Depression, to turn things around. Even today, the country still struggles with the question of when to intervene and how to allocate resources to deal with the problem.

Social Security Act of 1935

The Social Security Act of 1935 provided the first unifying national policy addressing children's basic needs for food, clothing, housing, and protection. The reliance on state and local governments, churches, and charitable organizations to address these needs had resulted in fragmented and unequal services. Although services continued to be provided by these entities, a common desire emerged to ensure minimum standards for all children, and the Social Security Act was a significant development to this end.

Title IV of the original Social Security Act established the Aid to Needy Children Program (forerunner of what is now Aid to Families With Dependent Children [AFDC]), and Title V minimally funded services for children who lived in rural areas and for homeless, dependent, and neglected children who were in danger of becoming delinquent.

A fundamental provision of the Social Security Act is the strict requirement of confidentiality, which must be extended to all recipients, adults, and children. Policy makers recognized the potential for stigma attaching to persons receiving government assistance. There is a need to respect the extremely private nature of the problems that cause people to seek the help available under the act. Thus, from an early date, strict confidentiality laws governed services for children.

AFDC-Foster Care Act of 1961: Public Law 87-31

In 1961, 26 years after the minimal provisions of the first federal child welfare services program, Public Law 87-31 expanded the

AFDC program to include federal funds for foster care. The AFDC-Foster Care Program contained several key policy requirements. For example, payments could be paid only on behalf of children removed from their home as a result of a judicial determination. The requirement of judicial oversight was designed to "protect against the possibility of capricious removals" of children. The AFDC-Foster Care Program was made permanent and mandatory in 1969.

A glaring oversight in Public Law 87-31 was the failure to require government agencies to work with biological parents to overcome problems that led to removal of children from their homes.

Child Abuse Prevention and Treatment Act of 1974: Public Law 93-247

In the early 1970s the focus of federal efforts expanded beyond neglect, that is, beyond parents who failed to provide basic necessities such as food, clothing, and shelter. The Child Abuse Prevention and Treatment Act of 1974, Public Law 93-247, was the first national legislation to significantly address physical and sexual abuse of children as well as neglect. Public Law 93-247 created fiscal incentives for states in the form of grants for child abuse prevention programs and encouraged enactment of uniform child abuse reporting laws.

Adoption Assistance and Child Welfare Act of 1980: Public Law 96-272

The availability of foster care dollars under Public Law 87-31, combined with the child abuse reporting laws, contributed to the tremendous increase in the number of maltreated children being placed in foster care. Once removed from their parents, abused children tended to stay in foster care and moved from foster home to foster home, entering adulthood without a sense of permanence. Partially in response to the problem of "foster care drift," the Adoption Assistance and Child Welfare Act, Public Law 96-272, was enacted in 1980. This act is considered the basis for the "modern" child protection system in the United States, and it represents a fundamental shift from earlier policies that tended to reward agencies for removing children from their homes and placing them in foster care.

Prior to Public Law 96-272, the focus was on ensuring that government representatives provided victimized children with safe environments through identification, intervention, and substitute homes. The 1980 law required CPS agencies to make "reasonable efforts" to eliminate the need for removal of children from their home, or if removal was required, to make it possible for the child to return home. For children who could not be returned to their parents, the law required that a *permanent* home be secured for the child, with adoption being the preferred option and guardianship or stable long-term foster care for children for whom adoption was not a viable option.

Value Conflicts and Inconsistencies in the National Policy Framework of Child Protection

The statutory framework that governs child protection is problematic for child welfare administrators and the social workers who are ultimately responsible for carrying it out. Like other major policy initiatives dealing with sensitive human issues, the legal framework is based on deeply held values that sometimes conflict with each other, leading to program goals that are vague and subject to conflicting interpretations. For example, the principle that it is best for children to be raised by their parents may conflict with the principle that children have a right to be protected. The principle that abusive parents should have an opportunity to change their behavior may clash with the principle that children deserve safe, stable, nurturing homes. The values of privacy and protection against false charges of child abuse compete with the values of immunity for persons making reports of child abuse and with the children's right to be taken into emergency protective custody.

Statutory language makes reference to the duty of CPS to "prevent" child abuse, yet CPS funding and programs are directed not to prevention but to children who already are victims. Although child welfare administrators and social workers endorse *primary* prevention, that is, helping families *before* intervention is needed, primary prevention does not play a major role in the work of CPS agencies. Thus there are inconsistencies between statutory mandates and program implementation.

Among the families that meet the criteria for CPS services, some families go without due to fiscal limitations. Budget bills are passed by the federal, state, and local governments, and budgets reflect fluctuating revenues and political priorities. By contrast, program policies stay on the books until modified or repealed, regardless of funding allocations. Consequently, in an environment where funding is chronically tight, professionals who implement policy are forced to set priorities; triage occurs even though the law is silent on this issue. CPS is to be all things to all people, yet CPS does not have sufficient funds to fulfill its responsibilities.

Yet another source of ambiguity and conflict is inherent in the different criteria for intervention reflected in the child abuse reporting law (Child Abuse Prevention and Treatment Act of 1974) as compared to the child welfare services law (Adoption Assistance and Child Welfare Act of 1980). The reporting law casts a broad net and errs on the side of bringing children into the system. The child welfare services law, however, excludes all but the most severe cases, thus reducing the number of children in the system.

Social workers continually sort through these conflicts and ambiguities in the course of their daily work with parents and children. In a given case, a social worker's decisions may be construed as contrary to statutory intent. The fact that a child is removed may in and of itself lead someone with no knowledge of the specific circumstances to conclude that the CPS agency is "antifamily." A dissatisfied party to the case may make a similar allegation to satisfy their own motives. Conversely, when children are left in what may appear to be marginal homes, critics with no inside information are likely to accuse the CPS agency of failing to protect children.

Checks and Balances Inherent in the Child Welfare System

Because the statutory child protection framework is combined with the practices of the juvenile court, an elaborate system of checks and balances has been formed to mitigate value conflicts and inconsistencies and to provide safeguards against misuse of government power.

Juvenile court laws enacted over the years have resulted in adversarial forums for litigation of the competing tenets of child protection, family preservation, reasonable efforts to provide services, and permanency planning. Although specific laws, procedures, and practices vary among jurisdictions, the juvenile court hears from all parties to the case—at a minimum, the parents and the CPS agency. Typically, a dependency hearing includes the child, the child's attorney or court-appointed advocate, the parent(s), the parent's attorney, the social worker, and a government attorney. It is not unusual for other family members, foster parents, and their respective attorneys to be present as well. Evidence is presented, witnesses are called, experts are consulted, and the judge makes the often difficult decision regarding whether the child is abused or neglected, and what services will be provided for the family. As is true with other judicial decisions, dissatisfied parties may appeal.

Thus the juvenile court judge, not the social worker, makes the final determination regarding whether or not the CPS agency will be involved in the lives of families against their will. This fact is often overlooked by critics of the CPS system.

The Bureaucratic Organization

Child welfare services are delivered by state and county governments. Although these hierarchical organizations are sometimes inefficient and impersonal, they provide a structure for review and approval of social work decisions. Any client of the system can ask for reconsideration of a lower-level decision, and can "go up the chain of command." Opportunities for review include frontline social work supervisors, middle-level managers, upper administration, the director of the agency, the county administrator, the elected county supervisors, and finally, the administrative agency under the governor of the state. In addition to the official chain of command, other government officials who have influence may be brought into the review process.

Critics of CPS express the view that the process for review up the chain of command is unproductive either because the agency "circles its wagons" and refuses to reconsider original decisions or because social workers retaliate. Although in isolated instances such totally inappropriate behavior might occur—and must be quickly and sternly dealt with when it does—the reality is that supervision by those in the chain of command goes on constantly. In countless cases, supervision resolves disagreements before they get out of hand.

Citizen Review Committees

Virtually every state and county has a number of citizen groups that serve as official watchdogs of CPS. Typical among these watchdog entities are agency advisory committees, juvenile justice committees, the local grand jury, a child abuse prevention council, interagency coordinating committees, as well as a number of ad hoc groups addressing problems of the moment.

In addition, advocacy groups exist in all parts of the country to support various participants in the child protection system. Typical among these groups are Victims of Child Abuse Laws (VOCAL—a parents' advocacy group), court-appointed special advocates (CASA—an advocacy group for children that provides volunteer services under the auspices of the juvenile court), and legal organizations that advocate for an improved system through litigation and legislative change.

Professional organizations also are involved in monitoring and improving the system. The National Association of Social Workers, the American Professional Society on the Abuse of Children, the National Center for the Prevention of Child Abuse, the American Public Welfare Association, the American Bar Association's Center on Children and the Law, and the National Association of Juvenile and Family Court Judges are but a few examples.

The Media

The media have shown increasing interest in the workings of CPS (see Chapter 7). Parents and others who are dissatisfied with CPS or the juvenile court can take their case to the media. The media can serve as a powerful check on abuse and incompetence by CPS. Child welfare administrators become frustrated when confidentiality laws make it difficult for them to respond to critical media coverage. Often, the "other side of the story" cannot be told. A successful strategy against this imbalance is education of the media and the public regarding laws governing CPS and internal rules and processes of the CPS agency.

Unfortunately, the presence of the media has created an environment that makes child welfare social workers and administrators extremely cautious in their decision making. Some argue that this situation leads to a failure to aggressively pursue difficult cases or to take the risk of trying new or innovative approaches in individual cases.

Responsible journalism should be welcomed by everyone within the child welfare system. When the media misrepresent, distort, or sensationalize the truth, however, or fail to give a balanced picture, CPS representatives should respond to set the record straight.

Interorganizational Collaboration

Child welfare services administrators do not operate their agencies in isolation. A high level of interaction with other organizations, community groups, and individual citizens is required.

Interagency cooperation is vital for many reasons, one of which is that many families are not eligible for CPS services. In fact, the vast majority of children referred to CPS do not receive services beyond the initial intake investigation. In California, for example, 90% of cases are closed at intake. Although most cases are closed early in the process, many of these families are experiencing difficulties. The challenge for social workers is to find voluntary public or private resources in the community to assist these families. Often, services such as parent education, respite child care, treatment for substance abuse, recreation, and counseling are needed. Although CPS does not offer these services directly to families who are not receiving CPS services, the ability to connect families with appropriate services is an important goal of CPS and is believed to prevent abuse and neglect.

Outcomes of CPS Services

The major federal reforms over the past 30 years have created a system that emphasizes the importance of (a) detection and reporting of child abuse and neglect; (b) the right to due process in decision making; (c) the need to provide services to protect children and rehabilitate parents; and (d) the selection of an alternate permanent home through adoption, guardianship, or long-term foster care when the juvenile court determines that parents are unable to provide a safe and nurturing home for children. An examination of how well these goals are met completes the framework for examining the backlash against child protection.

Child Abuse Reports Compared to
Children Eligible for Ongoing Services

The strong emphasis on detection and reporting of suspected abuse and neglect has resulted in a steady and sharp increase in the number of reports coming to CPS. For example, in California the number of reports doubled in the 7 years between 1976 and 1983, and doubled again in the next 6 years. California now has nearly 600,000 reports of abuse and neglect each year. Nationally there are nearly 3 million reports.

During the same time period, the percentage of children who received services beyond initial screening, assessment, and referral declined rapidly, a reflection of laws designed to keep children out of "the system." In California, more than 70% of children reported as maltreated received ongoing services before implementation of the Adoption Assistance and Child Welfare Act of 1980. Today only 12% are served beyond intake!

Court-Ordered Compared
to Voluntary Child Protective Services

Once a social worker makes an assessment that a family requires CPS services, the next decision concerns whether the parents should be offered voluntary services or whether the involuntary mechanisms of the juvenile court are necessary. The use of voluntary services as an alternative to court-ordered services varies widely among counties and states. Generally, the criteria for decision making include cooperative parents, maltreatment that is not severe (e.g., inappropriate discipline or inadequate supervision), and situations where the child can remain safely at home with agency supervision. The use of voluntary services for children who are placed out of the home is infrequent because (a) parents usually disagree with the decision to remove and therefore a court hearing is necessary; (b) the abuse is severe and court oversight is indicated; and (c) federal financial participation in voluntary foster care is limited to 6 months, and often it is not possible to predict the length of time needed to complete a rehabilitation plan.

In spite of limitations on offering voluntary services, there appears to be increased use of this alternative. Unfortunately, no data at the state or federal levels are available. A growing "family preservation" philosophy, combined with the adversarial nature of the court process, makes use of voluntary services an attractive option whenever appropriate.

Children Served at Home Compared
to Children in Out-of-Home Care

Whether services provided in the home are voluntary or court ordered, the first duty of social workers is to ensure children's safety while providing services to strengthen the family. This priority stems from the Adoption Assistance and Child Welfare Act of 1980, which emphasizes the goal of family preservation.

Although it is true that during the past decade the number of children placed out of their home increased nationwide, the percentage of out-of-home placements actually dropped. In other words, looking at the total number of children served by CPS, the percentage of children placed out of their home fell compared to the number served at home. This outcome demonstrates that social workers have improved skills for engaging abusive and neglectful parents in treatment and, as a result, progress is being made to avoid foster care placements and keep children safely at home, as required by law.

Placement With Relatives Compared
to Placement With Foster Parents

Another requirement of federal law is to give first consideration to placement with relatives when the juvenile court determines that protection of the child requires placement out of the parents' home. Here again, the fundamental value of the sanctity of the family is reflected in public policy. And once again, practice in the field reflects public policy. There has been an increasing use of "relative placements" over the past decade. In California, for example, two thirds of the growth in foster care between 1984 and 1989 is accounted for by growth in relative placements. Today, almost half of the children placed in out-of-home care live with relatives.

Conclusion

CPS has been given the grave authority to intervene in the most sacred of societal institutions—the family. Social workers are responsible for assessing the situation; determining if allegations are founded; providing direct services to eligible families; arranging services for ineligible families; recommending involvement of the juvenile court; monitoring progress of families receiving services on a voluntary or court-ordered basis; selecting alternative homes for children when the juvenile court determines the birth parents' home is unfit; and being accountable to clients, the public, administrators, and elected officials.

Do social workers live up to their responsibilities as prescribed by law? The evidence shows they do a remarkably good job despite ambiguous mandates, conflicting values, limited resources, and a plethora of critics who lack expert knowledge of the law and who second-guess complicated decisions.

Collectively, social workers respond to a huge volume of child abuse reports. In the vast majority of cases they quickly resolve problems or determine there is no problem. When further intervention is indicated they use their professional skills to enlist the cooperation of parents. When the juvenile court determines that a child cannot safely live with parents, social workers often find other family members to care for the child. Clearly, the day-to-day work of CPS reflects a system that is in tune with the wishes of the policy makers.

Do social workers make mistakes? Of course they do. Are there incompetent social workers? Yes, there are. Can social workers benefit from more training? Yes, they can. Child welfare administrators are responsible for ensuring that social workers achieve the goals with which they are entrusted. Human error and incompetence must receive immediate attention. Improving professional expertise must be a constant priority.

Manifestations of the Backlash From the Perspective of a County CPS Administrator

The backlash against child protection manifests itself in many ways, several of which are described below.

Attacking the Implementer

Social workers implement laws created by elected officials. Social workers are not at liberty to adjust or amend the law to suit their wishes or the wishes of others. Although social workers do not make the laws, they are too often blamed for laws that some view as antifamily. The law is complicated, controversial, and difficult to implement. Meaningful dialogue about the laws governing child welfare would be more productive than scapegoating social workers who act in good faith to implement existing laws and policies.

Rescue Fantasies

Citizens want *every* child to be safe. No exceptions. A child in need of protection sparks a desire to rescue. When children are abused and even killed, CPS symbolizes society's failure to protect its most vulnerable members. CPS is the obvious target for our collective guilt and frustration.

Lack of Incentives for Collaboration With Other Organizations

Because a well-run CPS agency necessarily involves a substantial amount of interorganizational collaboration, smooth mechanisms for cooperation are essential. Yet other agencies have their own sets of rules, priorities, internal politics, fiscal constraints, and value systems. Any of these, alone or in combination, can undermine interdisciplinary cooperation. If barriers are removed and replaced by creatively devised rewards for networking, infighting among organizations is replaced with mutual support.

Lack of Definitions and Data on Outcomes

There is little public awareness of what CPS social workers do, and even less knowledge of what they accomplish. Defining success in social welfare practice is problematic because the outcome that is right for one family is wrong for another. A certain amount of "failure" or relapse is inevitable. Moreover, some parents need periodic assistance to maintain an acceptable level of parenting. Because demonstrating success is difficult, the tendency is to document *the process* of providing services. Thus the emphasis is on how many visits were made to a family, how many referrals to other agencies were made, how many notices were sent, and how many court appearances occurred. As a result, child welfare administrators speak about high levels of activity within their agency, but they have difficulty clearly informing the public about what is accomplished. The difficulty of defining success leaves the door open for speculation about how well or how poorly the agency is accomplishing its goals.

How the CPS Administrator Can Respond to the Backlash

The goal of social work is to help clients solve problems. The social worker starts "where the client is" and builds a relationship of trust and credibility. This relationship is the key to helping the client define and overcome problems. The backlash may be regarded as a metaphor for the collective client of the CPS agency. In this framework, the administrator should reach out to the backlash rather than

recoil from it. The backlash provides an opportunity to build rela-
tionships with the fomenters of the backlash.

The backlash highlights the importance of strengthening ties with
allies who can provide support and guidance in dealing with the
backlash. The goal is to create a setting where competent social work
is recognized, where unwarranted criticism is dismissed, and where
mistakes are acknowledged. How can the administrator accomplish
these ends?

Communication With Service Providers, Parents, and Child Advocacy Groups

As an integral part of day-to-day work, child welfare administrators should reach out to colleagues in service organizations that
serve troubled families. Administrators should attain a thorough
understanding of other agencies' goals and methods of operation.
Likewise, the administrator should be available to the many advocacy groups that represent varied and sometimes conflicting views
regarding program goals, procedures, and services. Forums for
constructive debate should be organized.

The activities described above are not generally regarded as part
of the CPS administrator's responsibility. The heavy demands of
management *within* the organization can easily consume all of one's
time. Yet the demands coming from outside are equally important
if CPS is to be responsive to the public. Meeting both sets of demands requires knowledge, skill, purpose of action, and dedication.
In the words of the late Aaron Wildavsky (1988), "the public servants
who survive will indeed be a hearty breed" (p. 755).

Education Through Media, Ambassadorship, and Role Modeling

Because much of the public concern about child protection is
attributable to lack of knowledge about what CPS is and how it
operates, education is an obvious and important strategy for responding to the backlash. Unfortunately, there is truth in the old
adage that good news doesn't sell newspapers. Thus the media are
seldom interested in covering the day-to-day operations of CPS.
Nevertheless, administrators should foster good relations with reporters. Administrators can occasionally interest reporters in stories

about the inner workings of the agency. In addition, collaboration with the press is possible without compromising the confidentiality of individual clients and families.

Agency representatives armed with well-written, attractive brochures can participate in public awareness campaigns at schools, community forums, businesses, and churches. Town hall meetings to address specific issues help gain public confidence in CPS.

On a more informal level, every employee of CPS can serve as an ambassador to the community. Whether gathering with friends, visiting family, talking to neighbors, or the like, the subject of one's work inevitably arises. If the administrator takes measures to ensure that employees are well versed in the issues and activities of the agency, employees can share this information, respond to concerns, and become aware of new problems requiring attention. The expectation is not that social workers are on duty 24 hours a day. Rather, the idea is to empower them with information they can use to clear up misconceptions.

The behavior of the administrator is a powerful tool in communicating the purposes of the agency, its openness to dialogue on how to implement the law, and its responsiveness to clients. What the administrator does sets the tone for employee expectations. How the administrator interacts with others sends a message on how progress can be achieved. Seeking out support from allies, explaining the functions of the agency to a wide variety of audiences whenever the opportunity presents itself, standing firm on well-considered decisions in the face of political pressure, admitting mistakes, and being open to change are all part of good role modeling.

Research, Planning, and Quality Assurance

Positive media coverage and good public relations are grounded in accurate and up-to-date information regarding what the child welfare system accomplishes and what administrators believe is needed to correct problems and meet new challenges. Available data suggest that much has been accomplished, but much remains to be done. As is the case with many social programs, formal research is not an integral part of most CPS agencies, and planning takes place around yearly budget cycles rather than long-range goals.

Administrators are in a better position to address the backlash when they are armed with high-quality research data on the child welfare system and its operation. As technology improves and becomes available to public agencies, the possibilities for routine, comprehensive research increase significantly.

Mission Clarification

One of the greatest benefits of research on the child welfare system would be the ability for greater numbers of people to join the debate over child protection and to clarify what national, state, and local policies are and should become. There will always be disagreement over what is "best." Informed discussion, however, leads to agreement on common goals and promotes improvement in services.

FOUR

The Perspective From Victims of Child Abuse Laws (VOCAL)

LESLEY WIMBERLY

I first must address the title of this book, for it intimates that the "backlash" is against child protection. Given that the organization Victims of Child Abuse Laws (VOCAL) has long been dubbed as the "backlash" by those in the child abuse industry, I find this assumption incredible. VOCAL has never been *against* child protection. In fact, we support child protection. What VOCAL does demand, however, is a child protection system that differs from the way child protection is today. We demand that the child protection movement become a viable, professional, accountable system that truly protects children from all abuse, including the system abuse that is prevalent in today's child protection system.

Let's take a look at one small example of system abuse. According to a study done by the American Civil Liberties Union's Children's Project, abuse occurs with 10 times more frequency in foster and state institutional care than in the family (American Civil Liberties Union [ACLU], 1989-1990). Of course, this is not to say that all foster parents are abusive. But the increase in the numbers of children removed from their homes, and the decline in the number of foster homes, greatly increases the numbers of dependent children in each foster home, creating an overcrowded situation that breeds abuse and neglect. Because of this situation, the ACLU sued several states on behalf of foster children. Children suffering abuse in foster care are lucky if their caseworker can intervene, because of the immense caseload of each worker—a caseload that has increased to the point that many workers cannot make face-to-face contact with each child on a regular basis.

Other abuses within the system are complex. Many problems in the system result from laws that are hastily written and poorly thought out. As Richard Wexler (1990) writes in *Wounded Innocents: The Real Victims of the War Against Child Abuse:*

> The war against child abuse has become a war against children. Every year, we let hundreds of children die, force thousands more to live with strangers, and throw a million innocent families into chaos. We call this "child protection." . . .
>
> Believing that only the most brutal parental conduct was affected—so obviously the law only affected them and not us—Americans eagerly surrendered their most fundamental liberties to the child savers.
>
> We have turned almost everyone who deals with children in the course of his or her work into an informer, required to report any suspicion of any form of child maltreatment, and we have encouraged the general public to do the same. We have allowed such reports to be made anonymously, making the system a potent tool for harassment.
>
> We allow untrained, inexperienced, sometimes incompetent workers to label parents as abusers and even to remove children from their homes entirely on their own authority.
>
> We have drastically lowered the traditional burdens of proof and relaxed the standards of evidence used during the investigative process and in court.
>
> We have effectively repealed the Fourth Amendment, which protects both parents and the children against unreasonable searches and seizures.
>
> We have severely eroded the Fourteenth Amendment, which guarantees parents and the children that they will not be deprived of their liberty without due process of law.
>
> And we have foregone even more fundamental rights. After she botched the famous "mass molestation" case in Jordan, Minnesota, prosecutor Kathleen Morris declared herself, "sick to death of things like the presumption of innocence." She needn't worry. In the real world of American justice that presumption has always been difficult to maintain. In child abuse cases, it's dead. (pp. 175-176)

Wexler's book is only one of many describing the nightmare of false accusations and the immense problems in the child protection movement. Most of these books are written not by VOCAL members but by individuals outside our movement who are shocked, appalled, and angry about the state of the child welfare/protection system today. Unless all of us move forward through dialogue to improve the system, child protection risks being entirely dismantled by an angry public, a public that has placed an immense amount of trust and responsibility in a handful of dedicated people who can not keep up with the workload, let alone run a tidy ship. If we fail to communicate, and if child protection agencies fail to improve their own condition, outraged citizens will withdraw their support, and once again children who are abused will face a vacuum in public policy.

VOCAL was founded in 1984 by parents who were falsely accused and who were considered guilty upon accusation alone. Most of those accusations were based on "suspicion." *Webster's Ninth New Collegiate Dictionary* (1985) defines suspicion as "the act or instance of suspecting something wrong without proof or on slight evidence: **mistrust** . . . a state of mental uneasiness or uncertainty: **doubt** . . . a slight touch or trace . . . *syn* see **uncertainty**" (p. 1189).

The founding members of VOCAL were falsely accused parents who were treated as guilty based on mistrust, doubt, and uncertainty. Based on suspicion alone, these parents' children were yanked from home, school, community, and family; placed in state care; and plunged into therapy for abused children, regardless of what the facts were or what the children said. The result, of course, was severely damaged families and children. Such injustice occurred in the early 1980s in many states. Unfortunately, although there have been some minor improvements, serious problems still plague the child protection system, and the VOCAL hot line rings day and night.

VOCAL took a close look at the problems encountered by the falsely accused. We examined the child protection system from beginning to end, from initial reporting to adoption. We interviewed and listened to those working in the system. We examined their training, qualifications, salaries, job environment, and abilities. We talked with professionals who work with real child abuse on a daily basis. We looked at the problems in the communities where abuse occurs.

VOCAL now sits on many government task forces and committees throughout the United States and Canada. We work diligently to put a human face on the falsely accused and to bring about an understanding that false allegations are every bit as damaging to the child as the tyranny of incest. Some of you reading this chapter know

VOCAL members. Some of you have even attended VOCAL functions. But some of you have not. There are some of you—the same
people who never make an effort to meet us or attend our meetings—who angrily attack VOCAL, accusing us of "being supported
by huge insurance firms" or "a vast network of pedophiles." People
who make such baseless accusations must learn that it is the present
child protection system that creates VOCAL's constituency—nothing more. We, in VOCAL, are concerned parents and professionals
who want only to improve child protection, not undermine or
destroy it.

The Law

At present, the laws on child abuse are vague, broad, and scat-
tered throughout the codes. Thus it is difficult for those who are not
legal professionals, and more important, for parents to gain even
basic knowledge as to what is and is not against the law. I have lost
track of the number of parents who have called the VOCAL hot line
to tell us, "I didn't know it was against the law to spank my child"
or ask, "Why didn't somebody tell me it is illegal to be too poor to
heat my house?" or "Is it really legal for the government to interrogate and strip-search my child at school, based on an anonymous
report?"

Part of the problem is that the system responds to mere suspicion
as if it were established fact. Based on suspicion, the system moves
into the family with a vengeance. There is no effort to maintain a
nonbiased investigative approach. Fearful of their own vulnerability
to criminal and civil liability, mandated reporters report absolutely
anything, without regard for whether the suspicion is strong or weak.
No one can blame the reporters. The penalties are fierce should they
fail to report the slightest concern or fleeting thought of abuse. They
can lose careers, reputations, income—in short, a lifetime of work.

Our court system is based on the presumption of innocence. The
burden of proof is on the prosecution. Once accused of child abuse,
however, an individual is treated as though he or she is guilty. There
is no more presumption of innocence. The burden of proof seems to
be on the parents rather than on the state where it belongs. Only the
most experienced, knowledgeable, and well-prepared defense attorney can vindicate the falsely accused. Costs to those who hire

private counsel average $80,000 in criminal cases and $20,000 in juvenile court.

Unfortunately, because of the expense of employing a private attorney, many poor people, minorities, and single parents are assigned an overworked and inexperienced public defender, whose specialty is usually pleading out the case. Many parents have called VOCAL with the complaint that, in spite of their innocence, they were instructed by their court-appointed attorney or public defender to plead guilty or accept the county's assumption that they neglected or abused their child. Parents are told that it is hopeless to fight false allegations.

Federal funds are appropriated for the states to "guarantee successful prosecution of child abusers." This again shows the bent or bias in this area of law, for to guarantee a "successful prosecution" is to assume guilt prior to trial. Although there are federal funds to prosecute, there are no funds to defray the cost of defending against allegations of child abuse.

Unlike other crimes, child abuse cases can occur in two or more courts. Law enforcement may decide an allegation is unfounded, or the parents may go to criminal court and be acquitted. Nevertheless, the parents may find themselves trying to prove their innocence all over again, this time in family court. Once vindicated in family court, they may be accused in juvenile court. An accused individual who holds a teaching credential or a medical, real estate, or insurance license; is a member of the bar; or is in the military may be faced with an administrative hearing regarding the same allegation despite the outcome of the court cases. If the individual survives all this, he or she still may face a civil lawsuit should the accuser decide to demand financial compensation. Each court process takes on average a year to 18 months. The time, financial cost, and emotional price for the falsely accused and their families are fathomless. The child involved in a false accusation is devastated.

At this time, nothing in law or policy protects innocent children from being victimized by false accusations, or protects children from being manipulated as a pawn in divorce/custody disputes. Some family court judges are enlightened enough to remove such children from their vindictive parent. For the most part, however, the mere allegation of abuse is so heinous that judges refuse to give custody to accused parents—however innocent. Awarding custody to the accused parent could taint the judge as sympathetic to child abusers—certain death to a career on the bench.

The final insult to those falsely accused is the child abuse central registry. This registry, or index, is maintained in California and other states. Under the reporting statutes of California, for example, law enforcement and social services are required to file a form with the registry naming the accused and the alleged victim. Once in the registry, a name is never purged unless it is withdrawn by the reporting agency. The accused person's name remains in the registry, even if the case is later dropped or dismissed.

The problems generated by the central registry begin with the different approaches used by agencies conducting investigations. Law enforcement seeks information that will withstand the test of probable cause for arrest. Thus, law enforcement weeds out many false allegations. By contrast, a child protective services (CPS) worker—whose job is to "protect" the child and "believe the allegation"—is satisfied with far less evidence. Thus, when CPS conducts the investigation, it is more likely that the case will be "substantiated" and a falsely accused person's name will find its way onto the central registry.

In Florida, a state child abuse index came under fire in federal district court. A federal judge in Tallahassee ruled in 1990 that aspects of the Florida child abuse registry were unconstitutional (Whalen, 1991). The court ruled that it was unlawful for the government to keep citizens' names on the registry without their knowledge. The court also ruled that it was illegal to maintain a registry that did not make provision for correction of erroneous records. VOCAL is now challenging state child abuse registries in federal courts throughout the country. If the government needs to keep such records to track suspected pedophiles and abusers, the records should be accurate, and the accused should have the right to view the records and correct errors.

Child Protective Services (CPS)

Those on the front end of intervention are, for the most part, untrained and inexperienced. Although some CPS agencies place experienced social workers in emergency response teams, most counties take whoever they can get to work in this most difficult field. In rural areas, these problems are intensified because the funding mechanism behind CPS is based on head count instead of community need.

As counties struggle with thin finances, caseworkers struggle with an ever increasing workload and bureaucratic demands for paperwork. This paperwork avalanche interferes with what workers are supposed to do: social work. In fact, even the job description for CPS has changed radically. Many of the children in the CPS caseload should be under the care of mental health, probation, or education agencies rather than child protection. Yet these children are placed under CPS because of severe cuts in other, more appropriate agencies. In short, CPS has become the answer to all problems. Shrinking budgets and community services, along with rising poverty, impact CPS beyond the already existing burdens placed on it by law. Such overtaxing of workers causes high attrition, further undermining efficiency. These problems radically affect the children and families CPS is supposed to serve and protect.

Unlike police officers, who are obligated to undergo periodic psychological reviews and counseling as well as screening for the effects of their jobs, social workers are not screened or psychologically evaluated in spite of the stress and traumatic conditions they experience in the field. VOCAL's files contain many cases where social workers' personal bias and even hatred toward individuals— particularly men, and sometimes the family unit or a specific minority—steers their intervention and shapes reports to the court. This bias irreparably damages the family, the juvenile court case, and most certainly, the child. Yet, even if such bias is proven in court, nothing is ever done administratively to these workers. To date, there is no complaint system by which the family or the community can report a worker who deliberately attempts to derail reunification, tamper with evidence and witnesses, or commit perjury. Social workers are completely and totally unaccountable for their actions or inaction, unlike law enforcement officers, who are held to answer to a qualified immunity standard. As the saying goes, "Absolute power corrupts absolutely."

The Families

When a false allegation of abuse is made, the natural and immediate response is to deny the allegation. Yet, the denial does nothing to weaken the presumption of guilt. The falsely accused are considered guilty, but "in denial." When parents refuse to admit the abuse that never happened, their child is forcibly removed prior to any court hearing, and the parents find themselves and their child in the legal quagmire called juvenile court. If the parents are poor, they face the revolving door of public defenders being pulled out of the hallways to represent them at each hearing. There is no continuity, and very rarely any justice. Such parents are usually told to plead "guilty" and to agree to parenting classes and counseling. Even if they faithfully comply, the social workers assigned to their case rotate and change, again undermining continuity. The end result usually is no reunification. Visitation with their children is usually for 2 hours a month by a soda machine in a CPS office hallway. The parent-child bond becomes seriously damaged, if not severed. Once again, without a forceful, skillful attorney, parents become a statistic in the system and nothing more. Even more tragic, so do their children.

Foster Care

The children, meanwhile, are locked in foster care and drift from foster home to foster home, their belongings in a paper bag or box. Although there exist some excellent foster homes, many are substandard and overcrowded. Under such crowded and continually changing conditions, abuse is common. Some children are raped; some even meet with disability or death. Usually, the abuse is perpetrated by other children in the foster home.

Foster care can have a terrible impact on a child's life. Anne Williamson, a former foster child in New York, states:

> You're left hanging, and you wonder: Is my mother going to come and get me? Am I going to be left here? What's going to happen to me? Who am I? Whose kid am I? Is this my mother? Is that my mother? They're not my parents. But she's not either because she never comes.
>
> When you spend your life going from place to place and knowing you're not going to be in any place for long, you learn not to reach out, not to care, not to feel. I knew that if I reached out to my foster parents or to the other kids or to schoolteachers or to friends in school, very shortly I would have to leave and never see them again—never even get a chance to say goodbye. . . . If you don't get involved you can't get hurt. And that was my revenge on the world. (quoted in Wexler, 1990, pp. 174-176)

In his book *Child of Rage,* Glenn Hester (1981) writes:

> I read from a statement I had prepared, beginning by briefly telling
> my story. When I told of being bumped from foster homes to orphan-
> ages to institutions—in the process being severely abused—a few
> eyes lifted in the hearing room. I told how my moving from place to
> place had destroyed my trust to the point that at age nine a psychia-
> trist had diagnosed me as a child who neither loved nor trusted
> anyone. I told of my mental disorders and my experiences as an
> institutionalized mental patient.
>
> "I feel I was suffering from mental illness caused by my ill-fated
> experiences as a foster child," I charged.
>
> Then I asked some pointed questions: "How is it that a professional
> agency, such as the one holding me in care, could allow such a chain
> of events to happen to me as well as to others?"
>
> "Why has no real investigation ever been made or criminal charges
> of child neglect or abuse brought against individuals in this agency?"
> (p. 181)

Why, indeed? VOCAL and others realize that the child abuse
inflicted by the state is overlooked and excused. But if a parent
perpetrates the same abuse, the parent faces charges that could lead
to prison. Who is watching the watchers? No one. There is no
accountability. Not for workers who can scarcely find the time to
visit their charges a few minutes a month, and certainly not for those
few who deliberately fabricate reports to cover that lack of contact.

Not only do children suffer greatly, but foster parents struggle
with short finances because the foster care system is top heavy, with
more funding going into administration than to children. In spite of
requirements limiting the number of children in foster homes to six
or eight, social workers desperate to place children send more
children into homes than is allowed, adding to overcrowding. Some
foster parents are poorly educated and are not screened by authorities. It is usually these foster parents who use the meager foster care
money to augment their own income, shorting the children of even
the most basic necessities.

Foster parents complain of having no information about the children's background or needs, and the dialogue between the social
worker and the foster parent is brief at best. Foster parents are also
at risk for false accusations. If children do not like a foster parent's
discipline, they simply cry abuse and are sent elsewhere, leaving

destruction in their wake. Most foster children are experienced in how the system works. Their survival physically and mentally depends on their savvy and creativity. The result is one less foster home, and more overcrowding.

Society: The Impact of Imbalance

Because of the lack of definition and public knowledge as to where to draw the line between discipline and abuse, parents face a catch-22. Children today know that to cry abuse holds a threat over parents and caretakers, including teachers, a threat that can be utilized as a weapon against any adult-contrived structure they dislike. Such manipulation is especially common among preteens and teens. VOCAL's files contain many cases in which children threatened that if a parent restricted them, they would phone CPS and report the parent for abuse. If the parent relents and allows the child to become delinquent and truant, the parent must pay for the child's illegal action. In Los Angeles County, for example, a single mother was forced to pay a fine or go to jail because of her son's involvement with a gang. The media never reported that the mother's attempt to discipline the boy was met with the boy's allegations of abuse.

Parents suffer false accusations from many sources. Teachers report parents because educators fear that to ignore any suspicion may cost them their job. Neighbors report anonymously because they dislike the children, the dog, or the parents' religion or race. Ex-spouses—even those who are not vindictive—are often hypersensitive to a child's reaction to their divorce, and the child's acting out is often misinterpreted as a symptom of abuse. Many falsely accused parents whose children are removed from their homes and later returned are outraged that not only did the government fail to apologize, but the parents were billed for the cost of the child's detention by the county. "Why should I pay for the government's error?" one single mother asked. "Now I am rendered bankrupt because of their mistake. I now have to go on public assistance, an additional cost to the taxpayer, and my children suffer with government-induced poverty." AFDC single mothers are hardest hit. Many neglect cases come out of poverty. Once the children are removed, the mother is left with no income at all, facing homelessness. Reunification is again defeated, adding to the taxpayer's burden to supply funding for foster care for each child.

Teachers are falsely accused. Many teachers have been accused of abuse by children to whom they assigned failing grades or who required discipline in class. Some teachers are accused by elementary school-age children who are confused about what constitutes abuse because the children have been exposed to misleading information in school-based "child assault prevention programs" (CAPP). Although these programs have been defunded in some states, many local school boards still provide them.

In one school district, there was a rash of accusations against teachers and a coach. VOCAL investigated and found that the teacher's manual prepared by the district encouraged teachers of young children to "provide nurturing" and to "allow children to sit on your lap during meetings with them or during reading." These teachers practiced that nurturing. Unfortunately, a CAPP program was presented by the local rape crisis center, and the women who presented the program were rape victims, not trained professionals. They had no training in early childhood development or the cognitive ability of children in their early school years. The script from the CAPP presentation portrayed a coach calling to a boy leaving school at the end of the day. The coach asked the boy to assist him with some boxes. The boy responded that he could not because he had to be home at a specific time. The coach pleaded with him and offered him money. The boy relented. As the boy bent over to retrieve the first box, the coach grabbed. The script ended and the volunteer told the children, "That boy was sexually abused. This is a true story." Many of the young children decided among themselves that any touch was sexual abuse. Subsequently, a number of teachers were accused, and two ended up on trial. The children stated on the witness stand that the "touch" that was the basis of the charges was on the child's hip or waist, and was construed by the child as sexual. The defense attorney offered the script of the CAPP as evidence and the jury found both teachers not guilty. The damage was done, however. The school district revoked the teachers' credentials because the allegation had "brought embarrassment to the district," and the school district lost two dedicated educators. Some of the teachers' colleagues are quitting education out of fear the same thing could happen to them. The money wasted by the county in the legal battle is a cost leveled on the taxpayers. The families of the teachers are rendered destitute by the immense legal costs they endured. If this were the only case of its kind in VOCAL's files, we would simply consider it one of the costs of war—the war against child abuse. However it is not the only case. VOCAL's Sacramento hot line rings 60 to 100 times a day. Each call is either referred to a local VOCAL chapter or a legal or mental health professional. The intake is lengthy; and if we shortened the process, the number of calls would increase.

Conclusion

VOCAL believes that for the child protection system to begin to work efficiently, three major changes must be made. First, training. Although states have training programs, most are too short to provide in-depth training.

The second essential change is providing services to marginally dysfunctional families, and doing so by truly offering families help—not ultimatums or demands to admit to something they did not do. Ultimatums are coercive, not helpful. A project in Maryland known as Intensive In-Home Family Services sends workers who actually assist the family with any number of needs. No longer do poor families face losing their children because they can't pay the heating bill. The workers have a fiscal allotment to pay the bill and turn the heat on, and they don't stop there. They go into the home and assist the family living on a meager budget. They really do social work. And by the way, the attrition rate among social workers in Maryland is the lowest it's been in decades. These social workers are doing what they want to do—help people.

The third essential change is that CPS must stop trying to be all things to all people. Policy makers and lawmakers must be made to realize that CPS cannot be everywhere and be an answer to all problems facing children. We must begin to bring about an equity in funding to the various agencies that deal with children's problems, including mental health, education, probation, and public health. We must start focusing on areas of vital need and stop spending valuable resources and personnel on marginal or nonexistent allegations.

Those of you in child protection carry a heavy responsibility. You also have tremendous power. Sometimes your power is like a sword that must sever a child from the only world he or she knows, yet a world that could harm or destroy him or her. It is the careless use of this powerful sword that causes waste and needless suffering, not just to the parents, but to the child. Such misuse of power could bring about the demise of CPS. VOCAL does not want to bring about that destruction. We live in a society full of poverty, crime, substance abuse, and throwaway kids. We in VOCAL know the pain of the sword you sometimes hurriedly and carelessly wield. What VOCAL asks is that we examine together ways to save children who know only suffering, and at the same time, give real help to parents struggling to do their best for their children. VOCAL wants to make child protection the profession it should have been in the first place. If we don't, we stand to lose everything.

FIVE

Backlash and Child Protective Services From the Perspective of State CPS Administrators

CHARLES WILSON
SUSAN CAYLOR STEPPE

> Child Protective Services is the only group of professionals which
> society will not allow to fail. Doctors lose patients, lawyers lose
> cases but the public will not allow CPS to fail.
>
> Betsy Cole (1983)

As Betsy Cole so well articulated at a Child Welfare League of America conference in 1983, society has no tolerance for error by public officials charged with the weighty responsibility of protecting children. If child protective services (CPS) fails to properly diagnose the presence of abuse or the risk of future maltreatment, we leave a child at the mercy of those who may injure or even kill the child. Failure by CPS may also expose other children to abuse. There is no margin for error. Erring on the side of "caution," however, has its own problems, including labeling an innocent person a child abuser, tearing asunder a family, or directing treatment services at a problem that does not exist.

To meet this impossible error-free standard, society has developed public child protection systems. Child protection must confront this mission—perhaps a "mission impossible"—with human beings who suffer all the frailties of our kind. Adding to the stress of child protection work are unfortunate realities of public child protection: low pay, low prestige, high turnover, and less than adequate preparation for a very difficult task.

Common Elements in CPS Programs

Although child protection agencies differ in many ways, they share common features that are embodied in federal law and reinforced by prevailing theories of child protection practice (see Chapter 3). All CPS agencies accept reports from concerned citizens and from professionals referred to as "mandated reporters." State laws provide confidentiality for reporters in order to minimize the risk of retaliation from angry and sometimes unstable individuals. To encourage reporting, the laws provide immunity from civil liability for reports made in good faith.

CPS agencies conduct investigations, interview children and adults, and confer with professionals who know the child and the family. As the facts emerge, the social worker assesses the risk of future injury and develops a plan to reduce risk and build on family strengths.

When children are in immediate danger, procedures exist to take them into emergency protective custody. In 29 states, CPS agencies have authority to remove children from their caretaker (Younas, 1987). In other states, CPS calls on law enforcement to take children into emergency protective custody. Before children are removed from their home, however, the federal Adoption Assistance and Child Welfare Act of 1980 (PL 96-272) requires CPS to make "reasonable efforts" to avoid out-of-home placement. Reasonable efforts can include the use of intensive family preservation, teaching homemakers, and providing day care, parenting classes, counseling, mentoring, and case management services. When removal is necessary, a judicial hearing must be held within a certain time. Once a child is in out-of-home care, states have procedures to attempt to reunify the family.

To accomplish these complex tasks, CPS agencies use a variety of organizational structures and staff. Many agencies use baccalaureate-level professionals. The starting salaries for these staff range from around $15,500 in Tennessee (B.A. level) to around $32,000 in Hennepin County, Minnesota (M.A. level) (Child Welfare League of America, 1992). CPS agencies offer training to varying degrees,

ranging from unstructured on-the-job experience to formal compe-
tency-based certification training programs in states such as Ala-
bama, Georgia, Ohio, and Tennessee.

Criticisms of CPS

Prior to the unleashing of the backlash, the most common complaint about CPS usually focused on the agency's failure to accu-
rately predict risk in individual cases. When children known to CPS
are abused, especially fatally abused, public condemnation is intense. Professional careers have been altered or ended because of
misjudgment in a single case. When such tragedies occur, the media
often look for an individual to blame. In many communities, workers who misjudge risk are vilified in the press and suffer adverse job
actions. In central Florida in 1989, for example, individual case
workers and their supervisor were indicted on criminal charges for
their misjudgments on child protection issues.

Ironically, the current wave of concern regarding possible overre-
action of CPS agencies runs in the opposite direction. Critics such
as the National Coalition for Child Protection Reform charge that
child protection workers are so fearful of leaving a child in danger
and incurring the wrath of the community that they now tend to
practice "defensive social work," wrongly accusing innocent parents (National Coalition for Child Protection Reform [NCCPR],
1992b). Other critics, such as Victims of Child Abuse Laws (VOCAL),
believe CPS intervenes too often, abusing its authority (see Chapter
4 for VOCAL's perspective). Concern and anxiety find expression in
the popular media, where authors charge CPS with serious failings
(see Chapter 7). Six of the most common criticisms of CPS are
described below:

A. CPS Does Not Adequately
Screen Reports and Accepts Anonymous Reports

Many child welfare professionals acknowledge that screening
reports for seriousness and reliability is a significant issue. Frequently, individuals reporting abuse or neglect do not have adequate information to fully describe the condition of the child and
the circumstances of the case. In the absence of critical data, child
protection is faced with a dilemma: Should we ignore the report

because it lacks specificity? Or should we check it out just to be safe? In many cases, CPS selects the latter option because social workers are loath to leave children in dangerous situations. To improve the intake process, some states use a statewide, centralized intake unit that handles all incoming reports. Although this approach eliminates the personal touch of dealing with a local office, it makes for consistency in gathering intake information and decision making.

States use various tools to aid in front-end interviewing and decision making. About half the states employ some type of risk assessment model that highlights areas of concern. Risk assessment instruments and similar types of criteria provide a common framework for intake decision making. There is credible evidence that use of a risk assessment instrument at intake results in a higher substantiation rate, indicating more effective intake screening (Flango, 1991).

The practice of accepting anonymous reports has been criticized because of the seemingly low substantiation rate for reports of this type (Flango, 1991). Although there is inadequate data on substantiation rates, existing research suggests that anonymous reports are less likely to be substantiated (Flango, 1988). There is clearly a divergence of opinion regarding the wisdom of accepting anonymous reports. To critics, the low substantiation rate for anonymous reports suggests the need to disregard such reports. Most child welfare professionals believe, however, that the key is not to ignore anonymous reports, but to improve the intake process. Although anonymous reports yield comparatively fewer substantiated cases, such reports are unquestionably the source of very real and sometimes life-threatening abuse.

B. CPS Confuses Poverty With Neglect

Attorneys who represent parents accused in juvenile court of child neglect are sometimes harsh critics of the system designed to protect children, arguing that CPS too frequently confuses poverty with neglect (Wald, 1975, 1976). This position is supported by the National Coalition for Child Protection Reform, which asserts that the "confusion of poverty with neglect is the single biggest problem in the American child protection system today" (NCCPR, 1992c).

There is no denying that low-income families are far more likely to come into contact with CPS than middle-class families, and the poverty versus neglect issue poses difficult and ongoing problems for CPS. Although lack of resources is not in itself a reason to intervene in a family, experience teaches that lack of resources sometimes causes serious harm to children (Pelton, 1978). Some parents who have no money for child care leave small children unattended for unreasonable periods of time. Some low-income parents make just enough money to be ineligible for Medicaid, yet they lack funds needed to pay for essential medical care for their children. Time was when more parents could turn to their extended family for financial and other help in rough times. Today, however, with one child in four poor and the social "safety net" in tatters, CPS is increasingly called on to intervene.

C. CPS Has Too Much Power

The authority of a governmental agency to remove children from parents strikes a particularly basic fear in many of us. The issue of government power appears in much of the backlash literature (see Chapter 7). The National Coalition for Child Protection Reform tells us "CPS workers have the power of God" (NCCPR, 1992d). Others echo this theme, going so far as to equate CPS to the Nazis (Family Rights Committee, 1992). The Families for Freedom organization in Chester County, Pennsylvania, describes CPS as a "growing monolithic power beyond the reach of the voting taxpayers" (Dunsmore & Dunsmore, 1993).

All states provide safeguards to ensure that CPS decisions are not made arbitrarily or without regard for the seriousness of the issues (see Chapter 3). In many states, CPS workers must confer with legal counsel or a judge before removing children from their home. In other states, a conference with a supervisor is required. In all states, the courts maintain a role in supervising decisions made by CPS.

The fear of some critics that bureaucrats will abuse their power provides fertile ground for the backlash. CPS has increasingly come under fire for what critics allege to be overzealous intervention in families. For example, a 1993 *Woman's Day* article paints a distorted picture of CPS, suggesting that CPS workers always assume that "until those accused of child abuse or neglect can prove they're not at fault, the [Department of Social Services] assumes they are" (Stapleton, 1993). Readers are warned about CPS, and are given what can only be described as irresponsible advice about how to protect children from protective service workers. Among the more disturbing pieces of advice are the admonitions to "avoid taking a child to an emergency room if possible" and "if you leave your children alone in an emergency, don't tell anyone" (Stapleton, 1993).

D. CPS Staff Is Not Equipped to Do the Job

Critics charge that CPS sends "untrained inexperienced, sometimes incompetent workers" with "near absolute power" into homes to "interrogate and strip-search our children" (NCCPR, 1992a). Many child protective services professionals share the concern about staff competence and training. The individuals who investigate child abuse complaints hold frontline, entry-level jobs. In most communities these critical professionals have a bachelor's degree. Some communities prefer master's-level staff. Some locations that prefer master's-level staff will accept a bachelor's degree, however, because it is difficult to find ample numbers at the master's level. Problems in attracting *any* professionals are particularly acute in rural areas.

As stated earlier, training programs offered across the country vary widely, ranging from Tennessee's intensive certification program to no more than on-the-job experience. There continues to be a lack of resources devoted to adequate staffing of child protection programs and training of staff.

E. Reporting Laws Encourage Frivolous Reports

As the number of reports of child abuse and neglect increased, so did criticism of CPS. During the 1980s, reports of child sexual abuse grew particularly rapidly. Some communities experienced increases of 200% to 300%. As sexual abuse reports increased, more middle-class individuals became embroiled in the legal and CPS systems. Many of these individuals have the financial capacity to mount a spirited defense.

The 1980s also witnessed the emergence of another phenomenon, the defense expert. A number of these professionals have become outspoken critics of the system designed to protect children. Richard Gardner, for example, emerged as an extremely aggressive advocate for change in the child protective service system. Gardner (1993) attacks the federal law that serves as the underpinning for the national CPS system, urging the elimination of "the federal immunity clause" for persons making good faith reports of abuse to CPS. Gardner argues that "immunity from prosecution is incompatible with the basic philosophy of our legal system." Gardner goes on to allege that "such immunity encourages frivolous and fabricated accusations" (1993, pp. A10). Gardner also wishes to eliminate mandated reporting laws. Reading Gardner's voluminous outpouring of criticism, one cannot escape a common theme: Gardner's examples of frivolous reporting constantly refer to "hysterical mothers," "vengeful former spouses," and "severely disturbed women." Gardner seems to lay the responsibility for "frivolous" reporting squarely on the shoulders of women.

Unfortunately, Gardner's proposals serve to confuse the real issues. When Gardner refers to "immunity from prosecution," people may think of criminal prosecution. Generally, however, there is no criminal immunity for individuals who deliberately make false reports. The immunity granted in reporting laws refers, for the most part, to immunity from civil suit. Moreover, the need for immunity is obvious. If professionals must prepare to defend a potential lawsuit every time they report suspected child abuse, few professionals will report. Gardner's argument to eliminate mandated reporting does not stand up to scrutiny. Those who use CPS for vindictive purposes or who are mentally ill—and there are such people—would be unaffected by elimination of mandatory reporting. Doing away with mandatory reporting would simply reduce reports from professionals.

F. There Is a Lack of Due Process Protection for Individuals Whose Names Are in the Child Abuse Registry

The child abuse registry laws in at least 27 states require notification of persons who are reported as possible perpetrators. Subsequent to notification, states generally allow alleged perpetrators to challenge reports either through reviewing relevant paperwork or through a hearing (Flango, 1991). Child welfare professionals are not opposed to notifying individuals about reports of abuse. Indeed, existence of a rigorous review system enhances the quality of fact-finding by subjecting the decision-making process to added scrutiny. The only negative aspect of notice and review systems is the cost involved. These dollars are well spent, however, if the notice and review system influences frontline and supervisory staff to take a closer look.

Child Protection Advocates' Response to the Backlash

Child protection agencies across the nation are affected by the backlash. The backlash has helped shape the political environment in which CPS operates and the laws that govern CPS. Criticism has encouraged self-examination and improvement. In some cases, weaknesses within CPS were known to insiders, but external pressure was needed to encourage change. Unfortunately, some CPS agencies react defensively to criticism, taking action to calm critics, yet doing little to advance the cause of child protection.

Child protection is accused of many things. Although most CPS professionals can do little about fundamental problems such as low pay and high caseloads, all of us must strive to improve the system. The power to protect children must be used judiciously. Every time a child protection worker exceeds his or her authority, is overly aggressive, or unnecessarily disrupts a family, that worker legitimizes the backlash. Child protection must become its own most critical evaluator, ensuring that the considerable authority delegated to child protection is used wisely.

We believe that in the United states today the vast majority of child protection professionals are doing a good job of balancing the protection of children and the rights of adults. Thousands of children are alive today because of CPS social workers.

Recommendations

1. *Constant and Critical Internal Evaluation.* Child protection administrators must constantly review their training, policy, procedures, supervisory practices, and the nature of their organizational cultures. When CPS is charged with abusing its authority, it is essential to examine the allegation objectively and to face problems head on.

2. *Do Not Become Defensive in the Face of Criticism.* Respond to criticism in a nondefensive manner. The first rule for swimming with sharks is: Don't bleed. When administrators react defensively to criticism, critics are empowered. By contrast, a calm, objective response minimizes damage. Complaints about training, workload, and performance can be used to garner needed resources.

3. *Policy Analysis.* Administrators must guard against "one size fits all" decision making in child protective services. Large bureaucracies often function with strict rules and regulations. However, rigidity can seriously damage child welfare practice, which must operate in a dynamic, ever-changing environment. In child protection the answers are seldom clear-cut. Rather, there are degrees of right and wrong. Child protection workers are required to balance many competing interests, including family preservation versus child protection, parental rights versus child rights, and family privacy versus the need to ask questions.

To perform well in the pressure cooker that is child protection, staff must have clear job performance expectations, policy guidance, adequate and ongoing training, objective and supportive supervision, and the freedom to exercise professional judgment. Administrators can structure the decision-making environment, but professionals must ultimately make the difficult decisions.

4. *Support.* CPS judgments cannot be error free, and when mistakes happen staff must understand in advance that they will be supported professionally and personally. Support is most critical when a child dies or is seriously injured. At this tragic moment everyone looks for someone to blame, and the professional responsible for the case deserves and needs support.

5. *Child Protection Decisions Must Be Based on Risk Assessment.* Children live in a wide variety of undesirable circumstances ranging from serious poverty and violent neighborhoods to inadequate or inattentive parenting. CPS must not confuse poverty with neglect, discipline with abuse, or less than ideal parenting with maltreatment. Rather, CPS must determine what places a child at risk and how serious the risk is.

6. *Child Protection Should Guarantee Alleged Perpetrators the Protections of Due Process.* If CPS removes a child from the home or takes other action that adversely affects the rights of an adult, the alleged perpetrator should have a forum *within* CPS to challenge the decision. Conversely, if an accused individual's identity is not made public, and if the individual is not otherwise harmed by a CPS decision, there is little reason to establish a cumbersome bureaucracy within CPS to ensure that everyone involved has an opportunity for a hearing. Such systems push the concept of "due process" to unnecessary limits and drain valuable resources away from protecting children.

In the final analysis, CPS must take charge of its environment, honestly examining criticism from any quarter and acting appropriately. This is not to say that CPS should capitulate to critics. Much of the backlash is exaggerated and without merit. Nevertheless, mixed in with the exaggeration are issues that deserve attention.

SIX

The Backlash in Europe

Real Anxiety or Mass Hysteria in the Netherlands? A Preliminary Study of the Oude Pekela Crisis

KAREL PYCK

By 1987, doubts about the effort to protect sexually abused children were well under way in Europe. Two high-profile, multiple-victim cases caused particular concern, one in England and the other in the Netherlands. In England the so-called Cleveland crisis arose when two pediatricians "diagnosed so many children as the victims of sexual abuse that the social services department and the court system broke down under the strain" (Spencer & Flin, 1993, p. 8). A public outcry arose amidst allegations of professional zealotry. An official inquiry was instituted under the leadership of Lord Justice Elizabeth Butler-Sloss (Butler-Sloss, 1988). Spencer and Flin (1993) observe that although the Butler-Sloss inquiry "criticized the doctors for the way they had gone about their work," the inquiry "clearly reaffirmed that child sexual abuse is a major social problem, and refused to accept the idea that the whole business had been a groundless witch-hunt" (p. 8). (For useful discussion of the Cleveland case see Freeman, 1989; Richardson & Bacon, 1991.)

AUTHOR'S NOTE: Translations in this chapter are by the author.

Media coverage of the Cleveland crisis and the Butler-Sloss inquiry was extensive. Some reporting was thorough and objective, although other stories were exaggerated and distorted. Franklin (1988) studied reporting on the Cleveland case and observed that "most newspapers simply quoted the Butler-Sloss report selectively to endorse their previous editorial line. The crude and simplistic reviews typically published in the press, conveyed little of the complexities which Butler-Sloss had so thoroughly detailed" (p. 64).

In the Netherlands the Oude Pekela case began in 1987, when two preschool-age children apparently disclosed sexual abuse by strangers. As the investigation progressed, more children disclosed abuse, and as the number of possible victims grew, so did skepticism. The Oude Pekela case, and the negative reaction it generated, is described in detail below.

In late 1991, the Enschede case caught the public eye. Enschede is a city in the eastern part of the Netherlands. A 12-year-old boy admitted sexually abusing well over 100 children (Koopman, 1992). Initially, press coverage in Enschede supported the children's allegations and condemned the perpetrator. It was not long, however, before critics began referring to Enschede as another example of mass hysteria, "just like Oude Pekela."

Meanwhile, across the North Sea, controversy was brewing in Scotland. Spencer and Flin (1993) describe what happened:

> In 1991 Scotland had its equivalent of the Cleveland affair when social workers removed nine children from four families in Orkney, partly on the basis of what other children had said who had been removed earlier. The case was said to involve "ritual" abuse, and attracted the widest publicity. When the families appealed . . . the Sheriff [who in Scotland is a judge] . . . ordered the children home. . . . Amid growing public concern, Lord Clyde, a Scottish judge, was appointed to hold an official enquiry, the report of which appeared in October 1992. This report contained criticisms of nearly everyone who had been officially involved, particularly about methods used for interviewing children, but no attempt was made to ascertain the facts that remained in doubt. . . . What had actually been going on, if anything, thus remains a mystery. (pp. 8-9)

In 1986 in North Wales, a social worker named Alison Taylor was working in a group home for children. Taylor discovered that children were being physically and sexually abused in the home; she brought the abuse to the attention of her superiors and was fired for her efforts ("Whistle-Blower Paid High Price," 1992, p. 4). The on-and-off-again investigation, which continued into 1993, culminated in several convictions.

Belgium's child abuse cause célèbre began in 1984 when a 6-year-old disclosed sexual abuse by his father. The little boy's parents had recently divorced, and the youngster claimed the abuse occurred while he visited his father. The case received extensive media attention and eventually became known as the "case of Notary X." The Notary X saga took innumerable twists and turns, and like so many cases that generate a backlash, ended in uncertainty regarding the initial allegations. In 1990, a book was published on the Notary X case (Koeck, 1990). The author describes the case from the perspective of the accused father, and the volume is vituperative in its criticism of professionals who believed the child's description of sexual abuse.

Cleveland, Oude Pekela, Enschede, Orkney, North Wales, and Notary X do not exhaust the lexicon of cases that have generated harsh criticism of professionals working with children. Similar cases exist in Ireland, Denmark, Germany, and other locations. Although each case is unique in many ways, together they evidence expanding European criticism of professionals working to protect sexually abused children. To increase appreciation of the complexity of the European backlash, in the remainder of this chapter, I examine in detail one high-profile case—the Oude Pekela crisis.

The Oude Pekela Case

Oude Pekela is a small town of 8,000 inhabitants in the Groningen province of the Netherlands, near the German border. In May 1987, two preschool-age children in Oude Pekela disclosed to their parents that they had been sexually abused by strangers. As the investigation unfolded over the ensuing months, more and more children described increasingly frightening sexual abuse. As time progressed, it became progressively difficult to tell what really happened in Oude Pekela. Were children abused, or, as some critics argue, was the town in the throws of mass hysteria over nonexistent abuse? Two strikingly different accounts of the Oude Pekela case are reproduced below. These irreconcilable versions of reality typify the polarization that evolved regarding events in Oude Pekela.

A Critic's Perspective on the Case

In spring 1989, Benjamin Rossen offered his version of Oude Pekela in the journal *Issues in Child Abuse Accusations:*

> Just over a year ago two boys aged 4 and 5, while engaged in exploratory sex play with each other in the bushes, sustained slight anal injuries. . . . The mother of the injured child discovered a spot of blood in his underwear and took him to the family physician, Dr. Jonker.
>
> Dr. Jonker suspects that the child had been raped by strangers. In cooperation with the city council, police and a psychiatrist, he arranged a meeting for the parents at the local town center. About 300 parents attended this meeting. . . . The parents were told that dangerous child molesters were operating in the village and that their own children may already have been abused. . . .
>
> Over the next few months streams of reports came in. At first children told of being given candy. This developed into fecal and urinary games, sexual abuse, vaginal rape, sadomasochistic performance, manufacture of pornography, burning with cigarettes, drug administration, bizarre rites and the sacrificial torture and murder of infants. . . .
>
> Since no pornography could be found, a hospital investigation revealed no physical injuries apart from the slight wounds on the first two children, and the stories of the child were seriously confused and at a variance with one another, the police declared the episode to be an outburst of mass hysteria. . . .
>
> [A] hard core of angry parents, apparently driven by Dr. Jonker, were getting media attention and demanding that the criminals be tracked down and punished.
>
> The Justice Ministry in Groningen responded by appointing a psychiatrist, Dr. Mik, to interview the children. His job was to separate the truth from the fiction. The police and the Justice Ministry knew that nothing had happened and felt confident that an expert would arrive at the same conclusion and announce it to the nation with authority. They were to be disappointed. Dr. Mik spent months questioning children— using all the very worst possible methods—and came out with the finding that . . . it is all true and worse than we imagine. . . .
>
> Unfortunately, Dr. Mik was accorded credence by many people, including politicians. Others declared him to be a fool. . . . This is a tragedy not only for the children who are being taught to believe that they have been sexually abused, but also for the nation. People are far less confident about dismissing "The American Allegations." Some people are afraid that "They just might be true after all."
> (Rossen, 1989a, pp. 50-51)

Thus Rossen asserts that the allegations in Oude Pekela were a product of professional incompetence and hysteria. Europeans are warned to avoid the "American" experience of rampant hysteria.

A Description of the Case by Two Physicians Involved

Fred Jonker and Ietje Jonker-Bakker are physicians in general practice in Oude Pekela. They became involved in the case a few days after the first children disclosed abuse and were examined by another doctor. Jonker and Jonker-Bakker describe what happened:

> The story starts with a mother who brought her child for a consult-ation with a general practitioner (not Dr. Jonker) because of her child's persistent anal bleeding. The physician confirmed the phe-nomenon without knowing the cause. Two days later the boy told his mother that a stick had been put in his anus and that some older boys and adults did bad things to him and others of his friends.
>
> Our [that is, Drs. Jonker and Jonker-Bakker] first contact with the case was five days after the first physician had examined the child. We became involved because the anal bleeding was persistent (Rossen refers to it as only a slight wound). The mother told us about the sexual abuse and about having informed the police. A completely different story comes from Rossen, who declares that we had started it all up.
>
> Because of police suspicions, more and more children were in-volved. That is, during their questioning, the children mentioned the names of other children—and there was growing worry among par-ents. To avoid mass panic and mass hysteria, the mayor of Oude Pekela took the initiative to organize a meeting with the police, physicians, and parents of children at the only school believed at the time to have been involved. Rossen was not present at the meeting, and his description is completely contrary to what was said and to the general feeling of the parents. The police described without speculation what was then known about the incident. A child psy-chiatrist gave advice on how to avoid damage to the children, namely that in any case the children should not be subjected to interrogation. The atmosphere was for the parents' reassuring. No-body who attended the meeting can recognize any of the details as contained in Rossen's descriptions of it. (Jonker & Jonker-Bakker, 1992, pp. 260-261)

When the two boys implicated 25 other children, 17 officers were assigned to the police investigation team, but that number was involved for a short time. . . . The total investigation time lasted 18 months but did not produce any incriminating evidence such as admissions by the offenders, photographs or videotapes although children reported being involved in film activities. During this time 98 children, 4 to 11 years of age, were interviewed. There was no possibility of all the children knowing each other, as they lived in different areas and attended different schools. Younger children (3 to 6) were implicated early, but eventually cases of older victims became known. Usable information was provided by 62 of the children, and 48 children gave clear statements of sexual victimization. (Jonker & Jonker-Bakker, 1991, p. 191)

Given the remarkably different accounts of Rossen on the one hand and Jonker and Jonker-Bakker on the other, it is important to ask two questions. First, do we know what really happened in Oude Pekela? Were children sexually abused, or, as Rossen claims, were professionals and government authorities responsible for instigating hysteria? Second, whether or not we are able to answer the first question, what can we learn from the Oude Pekela case? In this regard the media's response is particularly important because the broadcast and print media played an important role in the events at Oude Pekela.

A Chronology of the Oude Pekela Case

The following chronology is drawn from the extensive media coverage of Oude Pekela, supplemented by study of the relatively small amount of professional writing on Oude Pekela, interviews of key figures in the case, and examination of those original documents that are available.

On May 9, 1987, the parents of two unrelated children report to the police their suspicion that their 4- and 5-year-old children have been sexually abused (Groningen District Attorney, 1988, p. 2; Jonker & Jonker-Bakker, 1992; Groningen Police Tactical Investigation Team, 1988, p. 2). The police begin an investigation. On May 11, the parents consult Dr. Jonker to treat their child's persistent anal bleeding (Jonker & Jonker-Bakker, 1992; *Achter het Nieuws*, 1987). On May 13 and 14, 1987, two local newspapers report on the investigation (*Nieuwsblad van het Noorden* [NN], 1987a, p. 1; *Winschoter Courant* [WC], 1987a, p. 3). The local district attorney confirms that an investigation is under way and states "that it concerns a very delicate case" (NN, 1987b, p. 3). The police state that at least 10 children may be involved, and parents are encouraged to watch for unusual behavior in their children and to contact the authorities (NN, 1987b, p. 3). The mayor of Oude Pekela calls an informational meeting attended by parents, teachers, and the authorities. On May 15, a spokesperson for the police states, "As we look at it now, we think it is more a question of child abuse rather than sexual games" (NN, 1987c, p. 1). Rumors develop that in a neighboring town several children may have been approached sexually (WC, 1987b). The authorities quickly squelch the rumors. The mayor of Oude Pekela states that the investigation continues (NN, 1987d, p. 17).

On May 25, 1987, the words "mass hysteria" are seen in print for the first time. Oddly, it is a spokesperson for the Justice Department, who says, "It is sensible not to worry people without need. Mass hysteria could easily be provoked, which I find highly undesirable" (NN, 1987e). Also on May 25, a police spokesperson says that "something really happened to the Oude Pekela children, and it absolutely was not performed by older children but by adults" (WC, 1987c).

On June 6, 1987, two local newspapers describe a police press release stating that 40 or 50 children are involved in the sex abuse case in Oude Pekela (NN, 1987f; WC, 1987d). For the first time, the national television station describes the case. Three days later, Oude Pekela is on the front page of all the national newspapers (e.g., Phylipsen, 1987a, p. 1). The most influential newspaper in the Netherlands, the NRC/Handelsblad ([NRC], 1987), runs a story describing anal injuries in one child and cigarette burns in two others (p. 3).

Some parents are angry with the national media attention. One parent states, "The children just started to become quiet again, and this wave of national publicity now hitting our region does not help" (WC, 1987e, p. 1). On June 11 and 13, a local newspaper writes that the tabloid press "devours Oude Pekela" (NN, 1987g; Molema, 1987; WC, 1987f).

Many parents believe they have not been fully informed, so on June 10 the mayor organizes a meeting to bring parents up to date. The mayor also appoints a spokesperson to release information as it develops (Phylipsen, 1987b). At the informational meeting, the mayor tries to calm the population by saying that the perpetrators are probably no longer active in the town.

On the national political level, the Oude Pekela case is linked with the possible role of the Netherlands in international child pornography. On June 10, the Minister of Justice responds to questions posed by a member of Parliament concerning action taken by the Dutch government against export of child pornography. During parliamentary discussions the possibility is raised that Oude Pekela could be a source of child pornography. A television program shows how easy it is to buy child pornography in sex shops in Amsterdam and encourages the government to do something to discourage child pornography (Dalmolen, 1987). On June 13, the French newspaper *Le Monde* discusses the role of the Netherlands in distributing child pornography (Fralon, 1987). The English newspaper *The Star* "calls for an urgent need to tighten Holland's notoriously lax laws on child pornography" (McCartney, 1987). In Germany, the magazine *Stern* comments that Holland and Belgium are the hub of international trade in child pornography (Trunk & Stimpel, 1987).

On June 13, 1987, NRC prints a front-page story that, for the first time, casts significant doubt on the children's descriptions of sexual abuse in Oude Pekela. The headline states "Probably Psychosis in the Oude Pekela Sex Affair" (Abrahamse, 1987a, p. 1). The reporter asserts that the district attorney in Groningen does not rule out the possibility of mass psychosis. Two days later, the district attorney responds in the newspaper *De Volkskrant*, where he denies that Oude Pekela is a result of hysteria. The district attorney states that the word "mass psychosis" did not come from his mouth but from the reporter's (*De Volkskrant*, 1987). In another newspaper the district attorney is quoted as saying that the allegations in Oude Pekela are "not at all a case of mass psychosis" (WC, 1987g).

The NRC reporter who first raised the specter of mass psychosis continues this theme on June 18, 1987, writing that Professor Marten Brouwer of the University of Amsterdam, an authority on mass psychology, believes Oude Pekela is a case of mass hysteria. Brouwer is quoted saying, "The way people react to the Oude Pekela events makes me think of the witch-hunts in the Middle Ages, mass hysteria" (Abrahamse, 1987b, p. 2). Brouwer compares Oude Pekela to the McMartin preschool case in Southern California and the multiple-victim case in Jordan, Minnesota, which, according to Brouwer, are examples of mass hysteria.

The chairman of Martijn, a society that defends pedophiles, declares "that he is afraid of a witch-hunt against pedophiles after the Oude Pekela affair" (Brunt, 1987, p. 2). The weekly magazine *Elsevier* takes up the mass hysteria banner (Abrahams, June 20, 1987, p. 20), and the newspaper *Het Parool* declares that "there was a mass psychosis between the journalists that week in Oude Pekela: hundreds of 'paparazzi' looking for a ghost! Poor children" (Brunt, 1987, p. 2). Journalists visiting Oude Pekela describe the anger of the citizens about accusations of mass hysteria. One resident says, "We people of Oude Pekela are too matter of fact for mass hysteria" (Kleijwegh, 1987, p. 9).

On June 18, 1987, it is announced that the Justice Department has appointed the child psychiatrist Gerrit Mik as an independent expert "to separate truth from fiction" in Oude Pekela (Abrahamse, 1987b, p. 2). Mik has sufficient time to devote to the case because he recently retired from the faculty of psychiatry at the State University of Groningen. During the 1980s, Mik was active in Dutch politics and was a member of Parliament. As a politician, he played an active role in supporting laws to protect children from sexual abuse. In Oude Pekela, he begins the long process of interviewing the children.

On January 10, 1988, a group of angry Oude Pekela parents distribute a pamphlet describing the sexual abuse of their children and expressing dissatisfaction with the official investigation. On January 12, a father (43) and son (25) are arrested and interrogated about their possible role in the case. After two days of questioning, they are released because of insufficient evidence. Some citizens are so outraged by the release that the father and son require police protection.

On January 16, 1988, the NRC announces that Mik "doubts if there was really sexual abuse in Oude Pekela" (Abrahamse, 1988a, p. 1). The newspaper states that Mik's report indicates that 40 or more children were traumatized but that sexual abuse is not certain. On January 18, however, Mik denies the newspaper story and asserts he never had contact with the newspaper about his report (WC, 1988a, p. 1). On January 19, NRC corrects its earlier statement, writing that Mik "suspects sexual abuse in children in Oude Pekela" (Abrahamse, 1988b, p. 3).

On January 21, 1988, the mayor of Oude Pekela convenes an informational meeting. At the meeting the district attorney states that the investigation will go forward. The district attorney describes what is known:

> The first complaint of alleged sexual abuse was deposited on May 9th [1987] by two pairs of parents. During the next few weeks the number of kids possibly involved slowly rose to some tens. A total of 98 children, 3 to 11 years old, were interviewed. The statements of 62 children were used in the further investigation. Finally 48 statements

of children remained, speaking of clear sexual abuse, which they had either submitted to or been forced to perform on themselves or on others. Many of the children told about strong lights, lamps on poles, and seeing each other on TV. The Justice Ministry concluded that it was nearly sure that photographs and videos were taken of the children. Against 18 children violence was used. The child abuse took place over a period of several months. The Justice Ministry thinks that four people, two men and two women, were involved in the sexual abuse. Probably the children were nearby their own homes and were lured into a car—ice cream and candy were promised. In some instances the sexual abuse took place in "carnival-like" circumstances. (Groningen District Attorney, 1988)

Mik is also a speaker at the meeting. He begins by stating that at first he doubted the allegations of sexual abuse. Gradually, however, he changed his mind. Mik's remarks are reported in several newspapers, including *De Volkskrant:*

The children were abused in very different ways. The youngest children had to fondle the breasts of women and to suck the penises of men. Older children were obliged to play a threesome, sometimes they were approached anally, mostly together with sadistic elements like whiplash beatings. Photographs and videos were taken of all this. Dr. Mik explained also how he tried to find the truth: Sometimes he misled the children (e.g., there was a red car instead of the blue car the children had spoken about. The children reacted that it was not a red car but a blue one). He also spoke about the fact that he talked it over with his wife and that she gave him some ideas about how he could find the truth. He then explained why the children did not talk about the abuse: They were ashamed and also intimidated: "If you tell something at home, we will kill your daddy and mommy." . . .

Professor Mik further declared that mass hysteria or paranoia is absolutely out of the question here. At the end of his speech, he became more empathic: "I find it atrocious what happened to your children. I know I have spoken with some distance, but I preferred to do so because I am involved as a professional in this case. But if I should set my emotions free, I should be very angry. I can run tapes of the interviews with the children that will bring tears to your eyes. What happened is so strange; during the night I even dream about it." He concluded his speech with the words: "It is sad that these events hit the people of Oude Pekela. They are accused of mass hysteria. If there ever have been nonhysterical people it has been here. They behave very, if not too, strictly. They don't shout, they don't outburst. At the same time, I think this is their strength as well as their weakness." (Phylipsen & Tromp, 1988, pp. 1, 3)

Despite the meeting, parents in Oude Pekela are unhappy with the inconclusive investigation. Some parents insist that the national Minister of Justice come to Oude Pekela. On February 4, the minister visits the town to restore the relationship between the parents and the Justice Department. The minister publicly sustains Mik's conclusions and denies the assertions of mass hysteria. The minister promises that aftercare for the children will be accelerated. That evening the parents announce they will renew their collaboration with the Justice Department.

Although the Minister of Justice calms things with his visit to Oude Pekela, it is the calm before the storm. A few days before the minister's visit, on January 30, 1988, a member of the Dutch Parliament, Hein Roethof, gave a lecture for Martijn, the society that defends pedophiles. The next day the newspaper *De Volkskrant* carries the headline "Roethof Accuses Professor Mik of Moralism." The newspaper quotes Roethof as saying, "Mik adds to moralization of the worst kind. If somebody like Mik in the case of Oude Pekela emotionally speaks about the perversities committed to children, without being specific, he also adds, undoubtedly involuntarily, to perversities" (*De Volkskrant*, 1988, p. 81). According to Roethof, the Christian right wing from the United States has come to the Netherlands. Roethof argues that the government does not keep sufficient distance from the sexual behavior of citizens. On February 6, the newspaper reports that Roethof "defends only the rights of adults" (Souren, 1988, p. 23).

On February 2, 1988, Oude Pekela is discussed on a national radio program. Professor Brouwer states that Oude Pekela is a case of mass psychosis, or "mass mental insanity." Professor Corstjens, a law professor at the University of Nijmegen, asserts there was no reason for the Minister of Justice to visit Oude Pekela. The next day, numerous newspapers discuss the radio broadcast. One headline reads, "Dr. Mik Suffers From a Little Mental Insanity" (*Het Parool*, 1988). Another asks, "Why has the minister [of justice] to go to Oude Pekela?" (*Trouw*, 1988, p. 2). A third comments "Small town lost its senses" (*Algemeen Dagblad*, 1988). On February 4, 1988, NRC reports an interview with Benjamin Rossen, who the newspaper says "came to the Netherlands to write a book on the psychological consequences of child sexual abuse" (Nijenhuis, 1988, p. 3). Rossen declares that "what children are telling after some pressure does not have any particular value."

On February 5, 1988, Brouwer publishes an article titled "Mental Confusion." Brouwer describes what happened some hundred years ago when young children alleged sexual abuse by foreigners. The children falsely identified individuals as the perpetrators. The accused were arrested, tortured, and executed. Brouwer asserts that we see such witch-hunts today in England, California, and Oude Pekela. Brouwer concludes by criticizing Mik's contribution to the "hysteria."

On February 6, 1988, two weekly newspapers expand the accusations of mass hysteria. *Elsevier* elaborates on Brouwer's ideas (Abrahams, 1988), and Peter Hofstede (1988a), a sociologist at the State University of Groningen, describes Mik as "the Shaman of the North."

On February 12, 1988, the journalist Van der Meulen summarizes the storm of criticism unleashed in the short span of two weeks. He notes how Mik was praised in the press one week, only to be vilified the next. Van der Meulen describes his impressions of the people of Oude Pekela. He does not detect mass hysteria. "Walking around in Oude Pekela, I realized that such a thing as mass hysteria can be detected much better from a long distance, behind a writing table in an office rather than on the spot" (Van der Meulen, 1988, p. 11).

Van der Meulen interviews Mik and asks the doctor's thoughts about the critiques of his work by other academics. Mik cannot understand how these professionals can come to such conclusions without being informed about what happened in Oude Pekela and without reading his report. Mik says, "I read some comments in the newspapers about how to interview children, but I have done it this way" (Van der Meulen, 1988, p. 13). And what of the critique by Brouwer, who states that Mik himself is a possible victim of mass insanity? Mik says, "He must be a very brilliant professor, because he did not even get in contact with me before he made his diagnosis. A matter-of-fact person would have first investigated such a problem. For me it is a statement not worthy of a professor. My guideline always was to be as matter-of-fact as possible. I created a situation where children could feel safe to speak with me" (Van der Meulen, 1988, p. 13).

The wave of negative articles during the first weeks of February 1988 has a lasting impact on public opinion. Weekly and monthly magazines continue publishing articles that cast doubt on the Oude Pekela allegations. Criticism of Mik and law enforcement officials is particularly harsh. We observe a continuing trend in the media to publish opinions from experts who had no part in the Oude Pekela case. An example of outside criticism is an article by Brouwer and Rossen in *Hervormd Nederland*. The article is titled "The Netherlands Bend Under American Pressure: American Background to Oude Pekela: The American Oude Pekela Is Called Jordan" (Brouwer & Rossen, 1988). Brouwer and Rossen (1988) compare Oude Pekela to the multiple-victim case in Jordan, Minnesota. They compare Mik to Roland Summit of UCLA and assert that both psychiatrists contribute to mass hysteria. Brouwer and Rossen (1988) go on to criticize the Dutch prime minister for suggesting that the Netherlands model its child pornography laws after laws in the United States.

On the first anniversary of the Oude Pekela case, Hofstede (1988b) publishes an article that disputes what the children said and casts blame on Jonker, Jonker-Bakker, and Mik for questioning the children in a suggestive and leading manner. According to Hofstede, the case involves nothing more than adult misinterpretation of innocent sex play between young children: "toddlers who poke each other with a twig from behind" (p. 25). Jonker is blamed for overreacting to what Hofstede claims were "slight anal injuries." Recall that Jonker, who unlike Hofstede actually examined the children, diagnosed persistent anal bleeding. Hofstede opines that Jonker "cooked up" the possibility the children were subjected to child pornography.

On October 18, 1988, it is announced in all the newspapers that the police investigation in Oude Pekela will end. Most parents react with resignation (WC, 1988b). Although the investigation has ended, criticism is far from over, and Rossen now positions himself at the center of the controversy. On October 30, 1988, a few weeks after visiting Ralph Underwager in Minnesota, Rossen appears on television and asserts that Jonker played an "evil role" in the Oude Pekela affair (WC, 1988b). In January 1989, Rossen publishes an article titled "Moral Anxiety in Oude Pekela" (Rossen, 1989b).

In January 1989, a few journalists question Rossen's academic credentials and motives. Pauline Sinnema (1989) writes an article on Rossen that begins with the headline "The Deceit of the 'Knowledgeable' Pedophile" (p. 2). Sinnema writes that the police in Oude Pekela refused to allow Rossen to examine files in the case. Kleijwegh (1989) writes that the official spokesperson in Oude Pekela did not trust Rossen. The spokesperson stated, "It was so clear, which way [Rossen] was heading. He only wanted to perceive what he believed. I advised the parents not to talk to him."

In fall 1989 Rossen publishes his book *Moral Anxiety: The Story of Oude Pekela* (1989b). In the first chapter Rossen writes that "the story of Oude Pekela is not a story about child molesters, because there were no child molesters" (p. 14). Rossen goes to great lengths to criticize everyone involved in the investigation. Rossen even reaches across the Atlantic to attack the FBI's Kenneth Lanning, an expert on child sexual abuse and the author of *Child Molesters: A Behavioral Analysis* (1987), written for law enforcement professionals. According to Rossen, Lanning's writing hardly meets the standards of the *Reader's Digest*. Lanning—who is respected in the United States as knowledgeable and objective—is blamed for spreading moral hysteria in the United States.

Rossen's (1989b) book is little more than an angry diatribe that is biased, poorly documented, and impossible to substantiate. Rossen indicates he spent more time in Minnesota discussing matters with Ralph Underwager than he spent on the spot in Oude Pekela. Nevertheless, the media is greatly interested in Rossen's book, and most journalists blindly accept Rossen's conclusion that Oude Pekela is a product of mass hysteria. The one-sided media coverage has its effect; and by 1993, Nanninga is able to state that "the case of Oude Pekela is generally considered in the Netherlands as a case of mass hysteria" (p. 13).

Thus, in the final analysis, an exhaustive 18-month investigation in Oude Pekela did not produce enough evidence to begin legal proceedings. There is little doubt that certain aspects of the investigation could have been handled more effectively. For example, some children were interviewed multiple times by the police, and some children were even interviewed in groups (Rogers, 1992). As in several of the multiple-victim cases involving young children in the United States, questionable interviewing techniques irreparably damaged the possibility of ascertaining the truth.

A small group of Oude Pekela parents petitioned the Court of Appeal in Leeuwarden to examine the way the police handled the investigation. The court concluded that the police had not done all they could to locate the alleged perpetrators. Nevertheless, the court concluded that there was not sufficient evidence to reopen the investigation (Jonker & Jonker-Bakker, 1992). Thus, although the police had left stones unturned, it was too late to do anything about it. Interestingly, the decision of the Court of Appeal—which can be interpreted as supporting the children's allegations—received very little press coverage. By contrast, Rossen's witch-hunt book was the talk of the town.

The Lessons of Oude Pekela

At the beginning of this chapter two questions were posed. First, what really happened in Oude Pekela? Second, what can we learn from this perplexing case?

In Oude Pekela, as in many other cases, it is impossible in the final analysis to know what really happened to the children. Despite the lengthy investigation, we probably will never know for certain how seriously children were abused by strangers in this small Dutch town.

Because it is impossible to prove that abuse by the alleged perpetrators occurred in Oude Pekela, it is equally impossible to rule out the possibility of mass hysteria. Indeed, proponents of the hysteria theory offer the inconclusive investigation to prove their point. Further support for the hysteria hypothesis comes from documented examples of group "hysteria" and from the societal tendency to discount allegations of abuse and to embrace less threatening explanations for children's allegations (Summit, 1988). Thus one lesson from Oude Pekela is that an inconclusive investigation can fuel skepticism about sexual abuse. In high-profile cases, therefore, it is important at the outset of the investigation to plan for the possibility that abuse will not be substantiated. Documenting carefully each step of the investigation thwarts after-the-fact allegations of improper investigative methods and mass hysteria.

The Oude Pekela case teaches us that in multiple-victim cases it is important to help the parents cope with feelings of anxiety and frustration. Parents should be informed on a regular basis of the progress of the investigation.

Oude Pekela highlights the importance of the media in shaping public opinion. Officials involved in the investigation need to speak with one voice to the press. In addition, it is important to respond quickly when erroneous information finds its way into newspapers and onto television or radio.

Finally, the Oude Pekela episode teaches the importance of examining the motives of those who speak out publicly about these kinds of cases. At the beginning of this chapter are two versions of events at Oude Pekela: one by Rossen (1989a) and another by Jonker and

Jonker-Bakker (1991, 1992). Rossen attributes Oude Pekela to mass hysteria, yet Rossen (1989a) is anything but objective. He presents only one side of the story and dismisses out of hand the possibility that there might be some truth to the children's statements. Moreover, Rossen's description of the early stages of the Oude Pekela investigation cannot be reconciled with descriptions in newspaper and magazine reports written as events unfolded.

What motivated Jonker and Jonker-Bakker (1991, 1992) to their conclusion that children were sexually abused in Oude Pekela? Unlike Rossen, these physicians were involved in the case almost from the outset. Jonker and Jonker-Bakker examined and interviewed children involved in the matter. Jonker and Jonker-Bakker's version of the facts coincides with early press reports on the case and with statements of the district attorney and law enforcement. Finally, Jonker and Jonker-Bakker's assessment is supported by the findings made by Mik, the independent expert with the most extensive firsthand knowledge of the case. Yet Jonker and Jonker-Bakker have a vested interest in their conclusions, and it is apparent that they have little regard for Rossen. For Rossen's part, the feeling is mutual.

I leave you to draw your own conclusion about whose version of reality is closer to the truth. Whatever your opinion, the irreconcilably opposed perspectives presented by Rossen (1989a, 1989b, 1989c) and Jonker and Jonker-Bakker (1991, 1992) reinforce the old adage, "Don't believe everything you read." Perhaps it is appropriate to add: When it comes to the opinions of outside "experts" who have no firsthand knowledge of a case, "Don't believe very much of what you read."

SEVEN

The Literature of the Backlash

JOHN E. B. MYERS

The human drama of child abuse attracts the media. Much of the writing on child abuse is emotional, reflecting the strong feelings aroused by the subject. Many articles, books, and broadcasts are laced with affect and tinged with hyperbole. Objective and balanced writing exists, but not in overabundance (e.g., Brannigan, 1989; Horn, 1993; Manshel, 1991; Ness & Salter, 1993; Whitman, 1987). In this chapter, I analyze critical writing about child abuse.

A review of recent newspaper and magazine articles, books, journals, and broadcast stories on child abuse reveals a disturbing trend: Reporting on child abuse is increasingly critical of the child protection system (e.g., Gelman, 1989). Coverage of child sexual abuse is particularly vitriolic. The deteriorating tenor of media coverage is well illustrated by comparing two magazine cover stories, one published in 1983, and the other a decade later, in 1993.

Dateline September 5, 1983: Time *magazine's cover story is titled "Private Violence: Child Abuse, Wife Beating, Rape."* The cover story contains a series of articles preceded by the headline: "The unspeakable crimes are being yanked out of the shadows." A series of articles covers efforts to come to grips with child abuse, domestic violence, and

AUTHOR'S NOTE: I wish to thank Michelle Ball for her valuable research assistance in locating the literature of the backlash.

sexual assault. The best way to get a flavor for the tone of the *Time* articles[1] is to read representative excerpts:

> It is beyond dispute that extraordinary numbers of women and children are being brutalized by those closest to them. . . .
>
> Today, the dirty secrets are no longer being kept. Victims of private violence are talking—to police, prosecutors, counselors, friends, one another—and U.S. society is trying to help. . . .
>
> The hard duty is to look straight at the problems and, neither laughing nor ranting, figure out what reasonable people can do. (Andersen, 1983, pp. 18-19)

> The wall of silence is breaking down even in cases of incest and sexual abuse of children by close acquaintances, which were almost always hushed up in the past.
>
> As abused children become adults, more and more are openly discussing their pasts, both to conquer their emotional problems and to help others deal with theirs. Private and government agencies are forming to aid the victims. . . .
>
> What the experts do know is that even the reported cases are far too many and that the cost in physical and emotional suffering, ruined lives and future crimes (studies of prison populations show that upwards of 90% of all inmates claim to have been abused as children) is intolerable in a civilized society.
>
> At stake is America's most precious asset, its human capital. At stake, too, is simple human dignity. If wolves and bears and birds take meticulous care of their young, why are human beings subjecting theirs to whippings and punches and sexual perversion? Children, with their unrestricted love and unquestioning trust, deserve better. (Magnuson, 1983, pp. 18-22)

The *Time* cover story expresses strong support for efforts to respond to child abuse. Criticism is reserved for the slowness of society's response, not for the child protection system. The *Time* articles typify much of the reporting a decade ago.

Dateline April 19, 1993: Things have changed. *Newsweek*'s cover contains a close-up of Shirley and Ray Souza, convicted of sexually abusing two of their young grandchildren. The Souzas' faces are filled with anger, bewilderment, and sadness. Next to them is the headline: "CHILD ABUSE: A court found the Souzas guilty of molesting their grandchildren. They cry witch-hunt. When does the fight to protect our kids go too far?" The cover story is titled "Rush to Judgment," and begins with the statement that "America is now at war against child abuse. But some recent cases suggest we may be pushing too hard, too fast" (Shapiro, Rosenberg, Lauerman, & Sparkman, 1993, p. 54).

It is illuminating to contrast the 1983 *Time* story with the following excerpts from *Newsweek*,[2] 10 years later:

> Americans are at fever pitch over child sexual abuse these days: we haven't done very well at preventing it, but we're frantic to root it out and stomp it to death no matter where it lurks—or doesn't. Woody Allen is accused, day-care teachers are jailed, women go on TV to describe their latest memories of childhood victimization. . . . Sometimes, amid all the noise, real sex abusers are identified and convicted. But too often, critics charge, the evidence is flimsy and the pursuit maniacal. . . .
>
> "This is a system that overreaches and gets jammed up," says Elizabeth Vorenberg, president of the National Coalition for Child Protection Reform, a group of lawyers, academics and others who believe that the current system ends up hurting children. . . .
>
> While it's rare for children to invent tales of sex abuse, some experts are convinced that in many instances children describe fantasies generated during months of intense questioning. . . .
>
> Psychologists who study the way children remember and recount events are building up a huge body of research on how easily children can be swayed. (Shapiro et al., 1993, pp. 54, 57-59)

What a difference a decade makes! Unlike the 1983 *Time* story, which spoke positively of efforts to protect children, the 1993 *Newsweek* article conveys a sense of pessimism and growing alarm that the child protection system is out of control and that many innocent people are ensnared in a system on a witch-hunt. To support its negative assessment, *Newsweek* gives voice to several of child protection's most strident critics, including Richard Gardner. In total, the article refers to eight professionals, with the work of six of them used to raise doubts about child protection. Thus 75% of *Newsweek*'s experts are critical. Finally, to drive home its thesis that child protection has gone awry, *Newsweek* ignores the many cases in which the child protection system works efficiently and concentrates instead on cases where doubts exist about professional practice. After reading the *Newsweek* article one is left with the distinct impression that the child protection system as a whole is out of balance and that action is needed to force the pendulum back to the center. The *Newsweek* story is emblematic of the increasingly negative media coverage of child protection.

In the remaining sections of this chapter, I describe the overarching themes and rhetorical devices of the emerging literature of the backlash and conclude with recommendations for responding to this literature.

Overarching Themes of Backlash Literature

Several themes dominate the literature of the backlash. These themes are outlined below, along with representative quotes from the print and broadcast media and from books and journals. The quotes convey the tenor and degree of the criticism.

The Child Protection System Is Out of Control

A common theme in the backlash literature is that the child protection system is dangerously out of control (e.g., Dean, 1993). In fairness to the critics, it must be acknowledged that the system is so overwhelmed that control is precarious. As the U.S. Advisory Board on Child Abuse and Neglect observed in 1990, there are "critical problems throughout the child protection system" (p. 31). In 1993, the advisory board reiterated its concern, writing that "the bottom line is that the child maltreatment crisis in this country is not being alleviated. It is worsening" (p. x). Yet backlash critics exaggerate the scope of the crisis. The critics assert not only that control is lost, but that the entire child protection system is on an irresponsible rampage. The following quotes illustrate this common backlash theme:

- The CBS evening news with Dan Rather and Connie Chung has a regular segment called "Eye on America." One night the segment described a San Diego man who was falsely accused of raping his daughter. The reporter refers to child protection as a system out of control. Moreover, the segment leaves the clear impression that false accusations are common.
- "The child abuse industry has spun out of control and become a voracious monster, hungry for human sacrifice, devouring everything in its path." (Eberle & Eberle, 1993, p. 408)

Frequent references in the media to a "system out of control" erode public confidence in child protection.

Child Protection as a Witch-Hunt

It is difficult to count the publications that draw comparisons between contemporary child protection and the Salem witchcraft trials of the 1690s. Indeed, one of child protection's most relentless critics wrote a book titled *Sex Abuse Hysteria: Salem Witch Trials Revisited* (Gardner, 1991). Quotes illustrate the pervasive use of witch-hunt imagery:

- "A climate of hysteria and witch-hunt mentality predominates." (Spiegel, 1989, p. 56)
- "Society was ripe for a witch hunt, nonetheless, and the accumulated energies poised to this end displaced themselves onto the virtuous cause of hunting for bodysnatchers of the nation's children." (Cockburn, 1990a, p. 20)
- "From the witch hunts of Salem to the communist hunts of the McCarthy era to the current shrill fixation on child abuse, there runs a common thread of moral hysteria." (Rabinowitz, 1990, p. 63)
- "The Salem Epidemic." ("The Salem Epidemic," 1990, p. 14)
- "VOCAL began smelling a witchhunt about two years ago, when the VOCAL hotline was flooded with a disproportionate number of callers who had been accused of child molestation in disputed custody cases." (Victims of Child Abuse Laws [VOCAL], 1988, p. 1)
- "The laws of this chase would have been the envy of the seventeenth century prosecutors at Salem." (Cockburn, 1990b, p. 190)

A writer hoping to capture attention is hard pressed to find a more riveting image than Salem. The temptation is strong to draw parallels between Salem and 20th-century child protection. In Salem, innocent people were convicted as witches and burned at the stake. Today, critics assert that innocent people are branded demons of another kind—child abusers—and imprisoned. In Salem, convictions were based on testimony from children. Today, children's testimony is the most important evidence in many sexual abuse cases. In Salem, children were repeatedly interviewed with leading and suggestive questions. Today, the media spotlight focuses on the way children are interviewed by social workers and police. In

Salem, the witch-hunt was permeated with religious fervor. Today, critics make similar claims.

On a superficial level, parallels between Salem and contemporary child protection are disturbing. Closer analysis reveals, however, that the analogy is flawed and misleading. In Salem, the women accused of witchcraft were, as a matter of objective fact, innocent. As far as we know, "real" witches do not exist. By contrast, many people accused of sexual abuse are, as a matter of objective fact, guilty. Unlike witchcraft, child sexual abuse exists. Thus it is misleading to juxtapose Salem (where 100% of the accusations were false) with child protection (where many of the accusations are true). The juxtaposition is misleading because it tempts readers to believe—incorrectly— that most accusations of sexual abuse are baseless.

In Salem, children's testimony was used to convict innocent people of witchcraft. Today, children's testimony is the cornerstone of child sexual abuse litigation. Although children's testimony is at center stage in the 20th century, just as it was in the 17th, it is misleading to compare Salem's children to today's young witnesses. In Salem the children were wrong 100% of the time. By contrast, children testifying today are often 100% right. To be sure, some modern children give false testimony, but comparison to Salem casts an unfairly negative pall over children's testimony.

In Salem, children were interviewed with suggestive questions that led them into false accusations. Today, there is reason to fear that improper interviewing leads some children into false accusations (Ceci & Bruck, 1993; Myers, in press). As with the other components of the Salem analogy, however, the comparison between then and now breaks down. In Salem, 100% of the children succumbed to leading interrogation. Today, however, children interviewed with suggestive and even leading questions often are accurate. The dangers of leading questions are as real today as they were in 1690, but it distorts reality to overlook the differences between what happened in Salem and what happens today.

Finally, in Salem, the witch-hunt was fueled by religious fervor. By contrast, 20th-century child protection is largely secular. This is not to deny the religious beliefs of many professionals working in child protection. There is no evidence, however, that child protection workers are disproportionately religious, and there is no evidence that child protection is infiltrated with religious zealots. In short, there is no reason to believe that religion plays a greater role in child protection than in any other calling.

The media's constant use of witch-hunt imagery undermines society's willingness to protect children. Lisa Manshel (1991) saw clearly the danger of the witch-hunt motif:

> It's ironic that a press drive crying "witch hunt" itself displays so many symptoms of being on a witch hunt of its own. The price we pay for this kind of coverage is the damage it will undoubtedly do to a societal awareness [of child abuse] that has been decades in the making. (p. 21)

The Child Abuse Hysteria

In backlash literature, hysteria is closely linked with the witch-hunt (Cockburn, 1990a, 1990b, 1990c). Indeed, it is common to find them side by side, as in "there is also an increasing, spiraling hysteria, fueled by some parents, therapists, and prosecutors—not unlike the emotional cyclone in 17th century Salem" (Hentoff, 1992a, p. 22). The following quotes illustrate the pervasive references to hysteria:

- "Invasion of the child savers: How we succumb to hype and hysteria." (Elshtain, 1985, p. 23)
- "The hysteria over child abuse." (Amiel, 1988, p. 5)
- "The national delirium over child sex abuse." (Rabinowitz, 1993, p. A8)
- "Many observers say the flurry of arrests and new laws aimed at easing the trauma of young victims sometimes misfires, creating a child-abuse hysteria." (Gest, 1985, p. 66)
- "Respectable experts say that therapists . . . are helping to stir a kind of mass hysteria." ("Satanic Abuse," 1991, p. 23)
- "The child abuse hysteria." ("Abusing Common Sense," 1990, p. 17)
- "The public hysteria on child abuse." (Spiegel, 1989, p. 58)
- "The U.S. appears to be witnessing its third great wave of hysteria. The first, the Salem Witch Trials, in 1692, lasted only a few months. Nineteen people were hanged before it became apparent that the accusations were suspect. In the 1950s, at the time of the McCarthy hearings, hysteria over the communist threat resulted in the destruction of many careers. Our current hysteria, which began in the early 1980s, is by far the worst with regard to the number of lives that have been destroyed and families that have disintegrated."[3] (Gardner, 1993, p. A10; see also Gardner, 1992)

Continual reference to hysteria undermines confidence in child protection by implying that many professionals are mentally unstable (Sowell, 1992). The image of hysteria is particularly dangerous because the image perpetuates discrimination against women. The majority of parents who make allegations of child sexual abuse are women (Thoennes & Tjaden, 1990), and many of the professionals in the field are female. In U.S. culture there is a long tradition of discounting women's allegations of sexual abuse and attributing such claims to hysteria (Olafson, Corwin, & Summit, 1993; see Chapter 2). The media's preoccupation with hysteria reinforces this legacy of disbelief and breaths new life into gender-based discrimination against women.

Professionals as Nazis, McCarthyite Persecutors, the KGB, etc.

Critics of child protection do not limit their portrayal of professionals to hysterical witch-hunters. Professionals are compared to other evildoers too (Gardner, 1993). The following quotes are representative:

- "Observers have likened the climate created by [child abuse] laws to that of Salem during the witch hunts, to that of Nazi Germany in 1939, or to that of the McCarthy era in the 1950s." (Emans, 1987, p. 740)
- "Questioning . . . kindred to 'brainwashing' in the Korean War." (Cockburn, 1990b, p. 190)
- "Elena Katz, a Russian emigre whose six-month-old daughter was removed from her home by New Hampshire social workers, yesterday called the Division for Children and Youth Services as brutal as the KGB." (Meersman, 1992, p. 1)
- On April 14, 1992, East Coast editions of the *New York Times* carried a full-page advertisement titled "Child Abuse Witch Hunt: The Rise of Fascism in Florida." The ad was placed by a Florida organization called the Family Rights Committee, Inc. In the ad, child welfare professionals are portrayed cartoon fashion as maniacal fascists bent on destroying families. In the last frame of the cartoon an elderly Jewish man with a serial number tattooed on his forearm gazes forlornly at child welfare professionals and says, "I've seen this before," an obvious reference to the Nazi persecution of the Jews. (Family Rights Committee, 1992, p. B5; for a newspaper story discussing the advertisement, see Rother, 1992)

To reiterate a theme that is echoed throughout this book, the child protection system has many faults. Tremendous efforts are needed to improve the system for children and parents. Is there any doubt, however, that rhetoric comparing professionals to the Gestapo undermines rather than improves the system?

Professionals Are the Problem

If the child protection system is out of control, who is to blame? Professionals, of course (Nathan, 1993; von Hoffman, 1992). Among the many professional failings are incompetence, zealotry, and corruption (Elshtain, 1985). Each professional group comes in for its share of criticism, although most of the venom is reserved for social workers, therapists, and prosecutors. Thus Alexander Cockburn (1990c) warns in the *Wall Street Journal* of the "cowards and opportunists in the justice system" (p. A17). Nicholas von Hoffman (1992) asserts in the *Philadelphia Inquirer* that "the child abuse scam is backed by the psychology industry" (p. 1).

Book-length critiques of the child protection system go far toward undermining public confidence (e.g., Wexler, 1990). In their 1988 book *Accusations of Child Sexual Abuse*, Wakefield and Underwager develop five themes. First, because children are developmentally immature, their allegations of sexual abuse are often unreliable. Second, many professionals who interview children use improper techniques. Third, the child protection system is flawed because "it evolved in the absence of factual knowledge derived from research evidence" (p. 19). Fourth, an unspecified but substantial proportion of professionals working in child protection are biased. Finally, an equally unspecified proportion of professionals are corrupt.

Wakefield and Underwager (1988) direct some of their harshest criticism at judges and prosecutors. They write that "an individual accused of sexual abuse of children can expect that the justice system will reflect the society's values and behave in special, unusual, and likely hostile, judgmental fashion from the moment an accusation is made, no matter what the circumstances or merit of the accusation" (p. 125). Wakefield and Underwager's distrust of the legal system is reflected in the introduction to their book, where Besharov (1988) argues that society believes alleged child abusers have "a lesser right to the presumption of innocence" (p. 5). Wakefield and Underwager (1988) concur, writing that "all agree that . . . accused persons are guilty" (p. 124). Wakefield, Underwager, and Besharov are not alone in this criticism. Christopher Fortune (1986) writes in *McLean's* that "parents are presumed guilty during the investigation" (p. 11). Hentoff (1992b) concludes in the *Washington Post* that "having been accused, Jim Wade was presumed guilty" (p. A19). Another *Post* article carries the title "Presumed Abusive" (Evans, 1991, p. B1). Although there is reason to fear that some professionals fail to respect the presumption of innocence, there is no evidence, despite the ranting of the critics, that this failing is the norm among professionals.

Wakefield and Underwager (1988) do not stop with the assertion that professionals ignore the presumption of innocence. They go on to write that some unspecified portion of prosecutors and judges find ways to "cheat, break the rules and obstruct justice in order to get a conviction" (p. 127). Wakefield and Underwager (1988) conclude their drubbing with sarcasm:

> Everyone knows that when people are accused they are guilty. When they are clearly guilty, the higher justice demands that the end justifies the means. Judges, prosecutors, and law enforcement have the moral obligation to do whatever is necessary to convict the guilty pervert because it serves their private beliefs about the higher good. It becomes a noble act to . . . obtain a guilty verdict no matter how it is done. This opens the door to all manner of rationalizations, justifications, and certainty that it is virtuous to do whatever must be done to win. . . . Exculpatory evidence is withheld or destroyed. Extraordinary effort is put into investigation and prosecution. Lies, circumvention, subterfuge, and hostile manipulation of legal rules abound. (pp. 130-131)

Wakefield and Underwager (1988) use vitriolic accusation to attack the motives, competence, and ethics of professionals. Granted, the child protection system is imperfect, and like all large bureaucracies, child protective services contains incompetent and corrupt professionals. Nevertheless, Wakefield and Underwager's relentless criticism does not ring true.

One of child protection's most ruthless critics is Richard Gardner, who seldom rests his prolific pen. Unfortunately, his pen is neither objective nor balanced. Thus, in his 1991 book *Sex Abuse Hysteria: Salem Witch Trials Revisited,* Gardner dispenses liberal doses of criticism to professionals in child protection. As for prosecutors, Gardner (1991) writes:

Prosecutors, like other professionals, exhibit a wide range of skill, from the highest to the lowest. I focus here on those who have contributed to the sex abuse hysteria described in this book. I recognize fully that there certainly are prosecutors who are not in the category described here; but there are enough in this reprehensible category to warrent [*sic*] my comments.

When a prosecutor concludes that no sex abuse has taken place, he (she) will enjoy little public attention. . . . In contrast, if the prosecutor finds that there is "suggestive evidence" (no matter how remote and preposterous), then there is "much work to be done." The uncovering process (often with justification referred to as a witch-hunt) demands significant attention as interested parties (and they are everywhere) eagerly await the outcome of the investigation. . . . In the process of the investigation, the prosecutor can gratify the same sexual urges described previously for the validators (vicarious gratification, reaction formation, voyeurism, etc.). But these benefits are intrapsychic and certainly do not provide notoriety. A young prosecutor, with no particular standing in the community, has an opportunity here to make a name for himself (herself). . . . Sex abuse cases in nursery schools and day-care centers make headlines. What a wonderful opportunity for a young prosecutor "on the way up." It is an opportunity for overnight fame. . . .

A prosecutor is basically a civil servant. It is a salaried position with the usual increments. In the crowded field of law today, the "best and the brightest" generally take jobs with prestigious law firms. . . . Civil service jobs are generally not those sought after by the superior students. Rather, they are more likely to be taken by those who have been less successful academically. This intellectual impairment is an asset when one is working as a prosecutor in sex abuse cases. It enables one to believe some of the preposterous things that they are told by the validators and thereby enables them to stay in the system and enjoy the benefits to be derived from such involvement. Other prosecutors, of course, are not justifiably placed in this category. They may be quite intelligent, but gravitate toward the work for other reasons—such as the potential for notoriety and the opportunity to gratify (in a socially approved way) sadistic urges via the deep involvement with criminal elements that the work entails. (pp. 103-104)

Gardner (1991) is equally complimentary of judges, writing:

In recent years I believe there has been a shift toward more opportunists and incompetents entering the field, and fewer idealists. I suspect that, at this point, there are still many idealists, especially at the highest levels, but I am convinced that the opportunists, incompetents, and those with less noble motives are very much on the [judicial] scene. . . .

Judges are not free from the psychopathological mechanisms described above for parents and validators. They too may have repressed pedophilic impulses over which there is suppression, repression, and guilt. . . . Incarcerating the alleged perpetrator may serve psychologically to obliterate the judge's own projected pedophilic impulses. (pp. 106-107)

Thus, among judges, prosecutors, and other professionals, we find unspecified numbers who are sadistic, incompetent, opportunistic, stupid, or pedophilic. Gardner (1991) himself assures us "there is a bit of pedophilia in every one of us" (p. 118).

On the scale of unbalanced critics, no one holds a candle to Paul and Shirley Eberle. The Eberles favor us with two books on child abuse. The first appeared in 1986 under the title *The Politics of Child Abuse*. On the dust cover the Eberles are described as investigative journalists. In *Politics* the Eberles warn of an nationwide witch-hunt in which innocent people are falsely accused of sexually abusing children. According to the Eberles, the false accusations come from confused and frightened children who are manipulated by corrupt and incompetent police, prosecutors, and mental health professionals.

For the reader who is familiar with child abuse, *The Politics of Child Abuse* is transparently devoid of objectivity. The book is little more than an angry and inaccurate diatribe. It is unlikely, however, that the Eberles intended *Politics* for informed readers. Rather, the book is targeted at the uninformed public. The danger is that the public will believe the Eberles.

The Politics of Child Abuse is a case study in exaggeration. The authors begin by exaggerating the number of fabricated allegations of child sexual abuse. Then they parlay the occasional overzealous, inept, or corrupt professional into an army of witch-hunters bent on destroying the American family. The Eberles (1986) ask, why are so many professionals "willing to destroy another person's life and family on false allegations of child abuse . . . ?" (p. 282). Answering their own question, the Eberles attribute the motivation to scoring "points toward a promotion, a pay raise, or a federal grant" (p. 282).

The most effective way to understand the Eberles (1986) is to examine their prose. In their concluding chapter they summarize their "investigation" of the child protection system:

We set out to unravel the mystery, and this is what we got: very little evidence of child molestation and a great deal of extremely corrupt behavior by police, prosecutors and "mental health professionals," resulting in the devastation of innocent people's lives and families. There has indeed been child abuse—perpetrated by representatives of the government and police, who kidnapped children, made them orphans, deprived them of vital family ties and trained them to falsely accuse their parents of high crimes. (p. 283)

Why so many obviously absurd allegations have been so vigorously prosecuted is an interesting question. Why are people willing to destroy others' lives for the sake of a pay raise and a step up the ladder of career advancement? Some do it because they are psychopaths. Some do it because they know their superiors require blind obedience rather than common sense and compassion. Mostly, they do it because they are scared. (p. 284)

That cops and others would use this weapon against innocent people—as they have done—in order to advance their careers, is a measure of their cruelty, and their depravity. (pp. 285-286)

The child abuse witchhunt was possible because we didn't learn anything from Joe McCarthy and his thought police in the nineteen fifties. The McCarthy era was possible because we learned nothing from Adolf Hitler. And Adolf Hitler was able to take power because we learned nothing from Robespierre, Torquemada and the witch hunters of the 1690's. (p. 286)

Venom drips from these passages. Nevertheless, one might excuse the Eberles as misguided zealots who unfairly magnify a serious but manageable amount of government and professional bungling. But excuses are not in order. There is reason to believe that the distortion in *The Politics of Child Abuse* (1986) is deliberate. Insight into the motivation behind *Politics* seems to slip out inadvertently while the Eberles are discussing the lengthy preliminary hearing in the McMartin preschool case in Southern California. The Eberles describe the seven original McMartin defendants as they sit with their attorneys at counsel table.[4] The six female and one male defendants hardly seem the type to molest children. The defendants are "pillars of the community" (p. 18). The women in particular "look surprisingly benign and gentle" (p. 18). It seems impossible that such respectable people could be involved in child abuse. To drive home the incongruity between the defendants and the charges against them, the Eberles (1986) write:

They are charged with what are generally viewed as the most loath-
some acts in the entire penal code. There may be crimes of greater
magnitude, such as murder and high treason, but none considered
quite as detestable. There may be some forms of deviant behavior
equally raunchy, but they do not embody the violation of the innocent
and defenseless. The acts specified here are not benign pedophilia. What
these people are charged with is the forcible rape of infants. (p. 18)

Benign pedophilia? The eye stumbles over the words. Do the
Eberles imply that some forms of pedophilia are harmless? Most
people consider "benign pedophilia" an oxymoron. Of course it is
important not to infer too much from two words in a book of nearly
300 pages. Perhaps the reference to "benign pedophilia" is an innocuous slip of the tongue or an outright mistake. When one studies
two of the Eberles' other journalistic endeavors, however, innocuous
explanations fade. In the 1980s the Eberles were associated with the
L.A. Star, a tabloid published in Los Angeles. The *L.A. Star* consists
in substantial part of advertisements for various sexual activities
and services. Interestingly, *The Politics of Child Abuse* was advertised
in the *Star* as the "best non-fiction book of the year" (*L.A. Star*, 1987).
During the 1970s, Shirley Eberle edited and Paul Eberle contributed
to a hard-core child pornography magazine titled *Finger*, which
featured explicit articles, photographs, and drawings of children
involved in sexual acts, including sodomy and sexual intercourse
with adults and other children.

The Politics of Child Abuse is portrayed as objective investigative
journalism. Yet, apart from an inadvertent reference to "benign
pedophilia," nothing in the book belies the Eberles' alignment with
child pornography. The Eberles' concealment of information that
most readers would consider relevant in assessing the merits of *The
Politics of Child Abuse* takes the book beyond inaccuracy and into the
realm of misinformation (see "A Strange Pair," 1988, for an informed
review of *Politics* from *Ms.* magazine).

In 1993 the Eberles published their second book on child abuse,
this one titled *Abuse of Innocence*. The book purports to describe the
trial in the McMartin preschool case. Again, the Eberles are described as investigative reporters, and again the book is an angry
and distorted misrepresentation of the child protection system. In
her review of *Abuse of Innocence*, Hollingsworth (1993) writes:

Ironically, the book itself is the grandest of all deceptions, from the title, which promises to tell the story of a trial, to the jacket copy, which promises to allow readers to reach their own conclusions, to the identity of the authors, who would seem to have a vested interest in curtailing the prosecution of crimes against children. (p. 6)

Thus criticism of child protection ranges from responsible to irresponsible, from accurate to wildly distorted. Yet the general public is not in a position to distinguish legitimate from illegitimate criticism. Average readers are as likely to believe the Eberles as they are to believe balanced reporting. The distorted literature of the backlash inflicts tremendous damage on the child protection system and, ultimately, on children.

Rhetorical Devices in Backlash Literature

Authors who are highly critical of the child protection system use several rhetorical devices to bolster their arguments, including scare tactics, making generalizations about the entire child protection system based on isolated cases of professional incompetence (Eberle & Eberle, 1986; Hopkins, 1988; Jones, 1993; Rabinowitz, 1990), and exaggeration (Cockburn, 1990a, 1990b, 1990c; Family Rights Committee, 1989; Lees-Haley, 1988). In some cases, the most vehement criticism is not from the author of the article—who may be trying to present a balanced picture—but from individuals quoted by the author. The following quotes illustrate common rhetorical techniques:

- "How the State Can Kidnap Your Children Legally." (Alliance for Family Rights, undated)
- "A wave of false allegations." (Coleman, 1987, p. B6)
- "For many parents engaged in seriously contested child custody disputes, false allegations of child abuse have become an effective weapon for achieving an advantage in court." (Gordon, 1985, p. 225)
- "Investigators and prosecutors [are] going after people with religious fervor." (Richard Power, quoted in Corwin, 1990, p. A26)
- "You're asking for a lawsuit, if not an arrest, today if you look crosswise at a child." (von Hoffman, 1992)
- "A fair trial was good enough for Charles Manson. Why not for Kelly Michaels and Raymond Buckey?" ("Abusing Common Sense," 1990, p. 17)

- "You're asking for trouble if you give your kid a bath without someone else's being there." (Katherine Sweeney, quoted in Lacayo, 1987, p. 49)
- "Don't touch that child. Don't work with children. Never be alone with a child. You have to look at every child who comes through the door as a potential threat." (The dean of a university school of education writing in a journal for teachers, quoted in Emans, 1987, p. 740)

Such strong language makes for gripping reading, but exaggerated criticism, repeated often enough, is misleading. These rhetorical devises are used in combination with the overarching themes of the backlash literature to convey a powerful message: The child protection system is dangerous, dangerous to children and adults.

Responding to the Backlash Literature

In view of the increasingly negative press coverage of child protection, professionals should encourage the press to paint a more balanced picture. Professionals need to increase their contacts with the press and should take time to write for the popular media. Academics, in particular, have a responsibility to devote more energy to writing opinion-editorials for newspapers, letters to the editor, and articles for popular magazines (e.g., Donovan, 1993; Carstensen, et al., 1993; Goodman, 1993; Herman, 1993; Myers, 1992b, 1993). Although academics contribute tremendously with their research and publication in scholarly journals, the public does not read arcane academic literature. Academics are uniquely positioned to contribute to the print and broadcast media because, unlike their colleagues in the trenches of child protection, academics have the luxury of time. It is unfair to expect overburdened practitioners to shoulder the responsibility for generating favorable media coverage.

Professional organizations focused on child abuse need to be more aggressive in "getting the word out." The American Professional Society on the Abuse of Children took a step in the right direction by creating a media relations committee and charging the committee to provide the public with balanced information about child abuse and child protection (T. Reid, personal communication, April 18, 1993; Reid is the executive director of the American Professional Society on the Abuse of Children).

The most important priority in reaching out to the media is generating positive coverage for our beleaguered child protective services agencies. Child protective services (CPS) social workers struggle under impossible caseloads, yet they are expected to make decisions that would tax the wisdom of Solomon. With little time to investigate, social workers must decide whether children have been abused, whether this child is safe at home, and whether that child should be placed in foster care.

Despite formidable odds, CPS social workers make the correct decisions most of the time. Oddly, however, when the child protection system works properly, no one hears about it! Social workers do virtually nothing to publicize their successes because confidentiality laws prevent them from discussing their work. Thus, when children are protected, the press pays little attention, politicians attend to other matters, and the public—which would rather not hear about 4-year-old rape victims and babies brain-damaged from abuse—is lulled into complacency. But let a social worker make a mistake and everyone is quick to condemn. Social workers are vilified as both incompetent zealots who snatch children from happy homes and inattentive bureaucrats who fail to protect children. County CPS agencies are the most important components of the child protection system, and they are getting a "bad rap" from the press. CPS deserves better.

CPS agencies may wish to employ a media relations professional. Although it is difficult to justify the expense of such a professional when funds are lacking to hire social workers, it is a mistake to underestimate the importance of good relations with the media, and through the media, with the public.

Confidentiality is important in child protection. Nevertheless, the complex web of confidentiality laws puts a counterproductive gag on CPS. Changes in confidentiality are needed so CPS can defend itself when unfairly attacked. Moreover, changes in confidentiality laws are needed so CPS can showcase its many successes. Finally, changes are needed to remove the incentive to hide mistakes behind the mask of confidentiality.

Generating favorable press for the child protection system is not easy. Yet the effort is vital. Critics of child protection are constantly knocking at the pressroom door. It is time for the professionals protecting children to pay a visit.

Conclusion

The print and broadcast media play a major role in the backlash, and it is important to respond to inaccurate reporting. Nevertheless, it is a mistake to become preoccupied with the literature of the backlash. True, some attention must be devoted to the critics of child protection, but most of our time and energy should focus on improving the beleaguered child protection system and letting people know the real story—the child protection system protects thousands upon thousands of children every year.

Notes

1. Quotes from *Time* are copyrighted © 1983 Time, Inc. Reprinted by permission.

2. Quotes from *Newsweek*, April 19, 1993, are copyrighted © 1993 Newsweek, Inc. All rights reserved. Reprinted by permission.

3. Reprinted with permission of The Wall Street Journal © 1993 Dow Jones & Company, Inc. All rights reserved.

4. I have no opinion regarding the guilt or innocence of any of the McMartin defendants.

EIGHT

Responding to the Backlash
Recommendations

JOHN E. B. MYERS

Each chapter in this book contains recommendations for responding to the backlash against child protection. In this final chapter, I will not recapitulate all these recommendations, but rather will pull together in one location selected recommendations that professionals may wish to consider.

Strengthening Child Protective Services

Child protective services (CPS) agencies bear the brunt of the backlash. Ways must be found to strengthen CPS. Much of value has already been written about concrete steps to improve CPS. This valuable work should not gather dust on a shelf. It is time to study this literature and take coordinated action. The reader is referred in particular to the following resources:

- U.S. Advisory Board on Child Abuse and Neglect. (1990). *Child Abuse and Neglect: Critical First Steps in Response to a National Emergency.* U.S. Department of Health and Human Services, Office of Human Development Services. Government Printing Office Stock No. 017-092-00104-5. This initial report by the advisory board contains excellent recommendations for raising the status and skill of professionals working in child protection.

- U.S. Advisory Board on Child Abuse and Neglect. (1991). *Creating Caring Communities: Blueprint for an Effective Federal Policy on Child Abuse and Neglect.* U.S. Department of Health and Human Services, Administration for Children and Families. U.S. Government Printing Office Stock No. 017-092-00104-5.

- U.S. Advisory Board on Child Abuse and Neglect. (1993). *Neighbors Helping Neighbors: A New National Strategy for the Protection of Children.* U.S. Department of Health and Human Services, Administration for Children and Families. In this provocative report, the U.S. Advisory Board challenges Americans to rethink our approach to protecting children.

The advisory board reports may be obtained by writing to the U.S. Advisory Board on Child Abuse and Neglect, 200 Independence Ave, S.W., Washington, DC 20201. Telephone: (202) 690-8137.

- National Commission on Child Welfare and Family Preservation. (1990). *A Commitment to Change.* To obtain this report write to the American Public Welfare Association, 810 First St., N.E., Suite 500, Washington, DC 20002-4205. Telephone: (202) 682-0100.

- National Association of Public Child Welfare Administrators. (1988). *Guidelines for a Model System of Protective Services for Abused and Neglected Children and Their Families.* To obtain this report write to the American Public Welfare Association, 810 First St., N.E., Suite 500, Washington, DC 20002-4205. Telephone: (202) 682-0100.

- American Bar Association. (1993). *America's Children at Risk: A National Agenda for Legal Action.* Chicago: American Bar Association.

Interdisciplinary cooperation is particularly important to successful child protection. Yet it is difficult to achieve genuine interdisciplinary cooperation. It would be useful to create economic incentives for agencies to collaborate with each other.

Parents accused of child abuse or neglect are the "consumers" of CPS services. No amount of improvement in CPS will cause accused individuals to view involvement with CPS as a welcome experience they would like to repeat. Nevertheless, it is important to ensure that parents feel they are treated fairly.

Virtually everyone agrees that one of the keys to improving CPS is training, training, and more training. Yet, is there a national consensus on what this training should be? If not, it seems the appropriate time to strive for consensus.

Finally, cultural sensitivity is a critical aspect of training for all professionals working with children and their families.

An Ombudsman for Abused and Neglected Children?

One exciting idea for improving child protection is to appoint an ombudsman for abused and neglected children. An ombudsman is "a government official appointed to receive and investigate complaints made by individuals against abuses or capricious acts of public officials" (*Webster's Ninth New Collegiate Dictionary*, 1985, p. 823). In Norway, there is an ombudsman (*barneombud*) to look after the interests of all children. Melton (1991) describes the Norwegian ombudsman:

> The concept underlying the Barneombudet is simple: It provides a voice for children's interests and acts as a watchdog to ensure that those interests are protected. Thus, the barneombud serves as a representative for children in policymaking and a guardian in policy implementation. The barneombud is not directly involved in making policy decisions but instead aims to ensure that children are able to enter the political arena and that, when they do, they compete on a level playing field. (p. 202)

In an important new book, *Establishing Ombudsman Programs for Children and Youth: How Government's Responsiveness to Its Young Citizens Can Be Improved*, Davidson, Coen, and Girdner (1994) describe ombudsman programs around the globe and offer concrete advise on establishing such programs.

An Inspector General for Child Protective Services?

Should child protective services (CPS) employ a high-ranking official to serve as an inspector general as that term is defined in the federal Inspector General Act (1978)? In the federal government, each agency of the executive branch has an inspector general who serves as a watchdog over the agency and is responsible for auditing and investigating the agency. The functions of a CPS inspector general could include:

1. Conduct audits and investigations relating to the operation of CPS.
2. Provide leadership and coordination and recommend policies designed to promote efficiency and effectiveness in the operation of CPS.
3. Keep the head of the CPS agency and the legislature fully and currently informed about problems and deficiencies relating to the administration of CPS and the necessity for corrective action.

To be effective, a CPS inspector general would have to be above the political fray. Perhaps the inspector general could be appointed by the governor and confirmed by the legislature. Appointment and confirmation should be without regard to political affiliation and should be based solely on integrity and demonstrated ability.

A CPS inspector general would report to and work under the general supervision of the head of the CPS agency. The inspector general should not report to or be subject to supervision by any other employee of the agency. Neither the head of the CPS agency nor any other employee of state or county government should be able to prevent the inspector general from initiating, carrying out, or completing any audit or investigation.

If the inspector general concept is considered, additional issues would need to be addressed, including:

1. How many inspectors general are needed in a state? Should there be a CPS inspector general for each county or region? Or should there be one CPS inspector general for the entire state? Answers to these questions probably depend on the population and size of the state.
2. The inspector general must have access to all files concerning CPS clients (see § 5 of the federal Inspector General Act, 1978).
3. Would the inspector general play a role in informing the public about the way CPS handles cases in general or about the way CPS responded to a particular case?

A number of states have laws that, to one degree or another, provide models for a CPS inspector general. The reader may wish to evaluate the following statutes:

- Arizona Revised Statutes Annotated § 41-1279.03 (1992)
- District of Columbia Code Annotated § 1-1182.8 (1981)
- Florida Statutes Annotated § 944.31 (1992 Pocket Part)
- Louisiana Statutes Annotated § 24:511 (1992 Pocket Part)

- Massachusetts General Laws Annotated, chapter 12A, § 7 (1992 Pocket Part)
- New York Executive Law § 48 (McKinney's Consolidated Laws 1982)
- North Carolina General Statutes § 147-64.5 (1991)
- Ohio Revised Code Annotated § 121.41 (1991 Supplement)

For information on state inspectors general, write to the National Conference of State Legislatures, 1560 Broadway, Suite 700, Denver, CO 80202. Telephone: (303) 830-2200.

Rhode Island's Office of the Child Advocate is particularly worthy of study.

- See Rhode Island Laws Annotated § 42-73-1 (1993)

Responding to the Literature of the Backlash

The popular media contains numerous articles that exaggerate the faults of the child protection system and undermine efforts to protect children. A more effective job needs to be done to respond to the literature of the backlash and to draw the public's attention to the many faults of the backlash literature. These faults include:

1. Lack of objectivity
2. Reliance on unreliable or biased "experts"
3. Questionable use of statistics

To counteract the backlash literature, professionals, especially academics, should devote more energy to writing for the popular media, including articles, letters to the editor, and opinion-editorials.

It would be useful to create a series of brief responses to the most common criticisms leveled against child protection. These responses could be furnished to the media. An organization such as the American Professional Society on the Abuse of Children could generate brief fact sheets on (a) prevalence of child abuse—what the numbers really mean; (b) what happens when a report of abuse or neglect is made; (c) issues relating to allegations of child sexual abuse that arise in divorce and custody cases, including information on false allegations; (d) what is known about ritualistic abuse; (e) what is known about repressed memory; and (f) what we know about children as witnesses, especially the suggestibility of young children.

Changes in Confidentiality Laws

Confidentiality laws serve important functions. Nevertheless, confidentiality laws sometimes create problems. Hechler (1993) writes:

> In theory, confidentiality laws are supposed to protect innocent adults and child victims. Sometimes, however, they protect no one but caseworkers and supervisors from unflattering publicity. When a family waives confidentiality, or when a child is killed and the parent is arrested and charged with the crime, why should the local social services department *not* be permitted—even required—to respond to questions about their prior involvement with the family? Why should they *not* be accountable? (p. 705)

> I am not suggesting that confidentiality rules serve no legitimate purpose, or that states and agencies eliminate them altogether. Social services agencies gather information from confidential sources for the same reasons journalists do: The guarantee of anonymity emboldens those who might otherwise remain silent. Furthermore, the cloak of anonymity shields child victims from stigma and affords accused adults at least some protection in a system that requires nothing more to trigger an investigation than the suspicion of a nameless citizen.
>   What I *am* suggesting, however, is that confidentiality should not be invoked by a public agency for the sole purpose of shielding itself from scrutiny. (p. 707)

> Too often confidentiality rules are used by agencies to prevent undesired news coverage. Lost in bureaucratic legerdemain are questions that demand responses. Does not *true* damage control require that agencies discipline incompetence—and let everyone know it? . . .
>   The real damage is not embarrassing publicity. The real damage is what results from a system accountable only to itself. It is a system that sometimes seems as self-contained as a mathematical equation, and one that is bent on proving this theorem: closed minds + closed ranks = closed case. (p. 707)

Changes in confidentiality laws are needed to:

1. Allow child protection agencies to defend themselves against unwarranted criticism.
2. Allow child protection agencies to showcase their successes.
3. Remove the incentive and ability of child protection agencies to use confidentiality laws to conceal mistakes (Grimm, 1992).

It may be wise for the juvenile court to oversee release of confidential CPS information.

Should the Public Be Invited Into CPS so Citizens Get a More Accurate Picture of CPS Work?

Would it improve CPS to invite the public to visit CPS agencies to see what "really happens"? Are there parallels to police ride-along programs and open-house days at military installations?

Professionals Who Exceed the Limits of Current Knowledge

Professionals inside and out of CPS agencies deserve criticism when they exceed the bounds of current knowledge. The problem of exceeding established knowledge appears to be particularly common when professionals provide expert testimony in court and when professionals misuse of statistics about the prevalence of child abuse.

More Effective Lobbying

The importance of effective lobbying cannot be overstated. Yet the critics of child protection appear to be "out-lobbying" the child protection community. Children's groups sometimes work at cross-purposes. Child protection professionals appear to be falling prey to the divide-and-conquer technique.

References

Abrahams, F. (1987, June 20). Fantastische vertellingen: De massahysterie over ontucht met kleuters in Oude Pekela. *Elsevier, 43*, 20-24.

Abrahams, F. (1988, February 6). De psychiater en zijn zekerheden. *Elsevier, 44*, 21-24.

Abrahamse, M. (1987a, June 13). Wellicht psychose in sekszaak Oude Pekela. *NRC, 17*, 1.

Abrahamse, M. (1987b, June 18). Hoogleraar noemt reactie op "Oude Pekela" massahysterie. *NRC, 17*, 2.

Abrahamse, M. (1988a, January 16). Psychiater twijfelt aan ontucht met kinderen. *NRC, 18*, 1.

Abrahamse, M. (1988b, January 19). Psychiater vermoedt seks met kinderen in Oude Pekela. *NRC, 18*, 3.

Abusing common sense [Unsigned editorial]. (1990, May 28). *National Review, 42*, 16-17.

Achter het Nieuws. (1987, June 12). [Dutch television news program].

Adoption Assistance and Child Welfare Act of 1980, 25 U.S.C. § 50B and 42 U.S.C. § 602 (Public Law 96-272).

Algemeen Dagblad. (1988, February 3). "Dorp de kluts kwijt." Woede in Oude Pekela na uitlating van Hoogleraar. *Algemeen Dagblad.*

Alliance for Family Rights. (undated). *How the state can kidnap your children legally.* (Available from Alliance for Family Rights, RFD #1, Box 140, New Hampton, NH 03256)

American Bar Association. (1993). *America's children at risk: A national agenda for legal action.* Chicago: American Bar Association.

American Civil Liberties Union. (1989-1990). *Children's rights project.* New York: Author.

Amiel, B. (1988, August 22). The hysteria over child abuse. *McLean's, 101*, 5.

Andersen, K. (1983, September 5). Private violence: The unspeakable crimes are being yanked out of the shadows. *Time*, pp. 18-19.

Arizona Revised Statutes Annotated § 41-1279.03 (1992).

A strange pair of experts. (1988, December). *Ms., 17*, 92.

Au, T. (1992). Counterfactual reasoning. In G. R. Semin & K. Fiedler (Eds.), *Language, interaction and social cognition* (pp. 194-213). London: Sage.

111

Besharov, D. (1988). Introduction: The central dilemma: Protecting abused children while protecting innocent parents. In H. Wakefield & R. Underwager (Eds.), *Accusations of child sexual abuse* (p. 5). Springfield, IL: Charles C Thomas.

Blumer, H. (1971). Social problems as collective behavior. *Social Problems, 18,* 289-306.

Brannigan, M. (1989, August 23). The accused: Child-abuse charges ensnare some parents in baseless proceedings. *Wall Street Journal,* p. A1.

Bremner, R. H. (Ed.). (1970). *Child and youth in America: A documentary history.* Cambridge, MA: Harvard University Press.

Brouwer, M. (1988, February 5). Het verstand vertroebeld. *Het Parool, 48,* 7.

Brouwer, M., & Rossen, B. (1988, March 5). Nederland zwicht voor Amerikaanse druk. Amerikaanse achtergronden van Oude Pekela. *Hervormd Nederland, 44,* 10-11.

Brown, M. (1926). *Legal psychology.* Indianapolis, IN: Bobbs-Merrill.

Brown v. Board of Education, 347 U.S. 483 (1954).

Brunt, L. (1987, June 20). Een nieuwtje in Oude Pekela. *Het Parool, 47,* 2.

Bussey, K., Lee, K., & Grimbeek, E. J. (1993). Lies and secrets: Implications for children's reporting of sexual abuse. In G. S. Goodman & B. L. Bottoms (Eds.), *Child victims, child witnesses: Understanding and improving testimony* (pp. 147-168). New York: Guilford.

Butler-Sloss, E. (1988). *Report of the inquiry into child abuse in Cleveland 1987* (Cm 412). London: Department of Health and Social Security.

California Welfare and Institutions Code § 16501 (1993).

Carstensen, L. L., Gabrieli, J., Shepard, R., Levenson, R. W., Mason, M. A., Goodman, G., Bootzin, R., Ceci, S. J., Bronfrenbrenner, U., Edelstein, B. A., Schober, M., Bruck, M., Keane, T., Zimering, R., Oltmanns, T. F., Gotlib, I., & Ekman, P. (1993, March). Repressed objectivity [Letter to the editor]. *APS Observer,* p. 23.

Ceci, S. J., & Bruck, M. (1993). Suggestibility of the child witness: A historical review and synthesis. *Psychological Bulletin, 113,* 403-439.

Child Abuse Prevention and Treatment Act of 1974, 42 U.S.C. § 5101 (Public Law 93-247).

Child Welfare League of America. (1992). *State public caseload survey* (Prepared by Patrick A. Curtis, Ph.D.).

Cockburn, A. (1990a, January 26). Abused imaginings: Tales of child sexual abuse, with overtones of the occult, have been rife in the US. But are they true, asks Alexander Cockburn. *New Statesman and Society, 3,* 19-20.

Cockburn, A. (1990b, February 12). Beat the devil. *The Nation, 250,* 190.

Cockburn, A. (1990c, February 8). The McMartin Case: Indict the children, jail the parents. *Wall Street Journal,* p. A17.

Cole, B. (1983). Speech presented at a conference of the Child Welfare League of America, Charleston, SC.

Coleman, L. (1986a, January-February). False allegations of child sexual abuse: Have the experts been caught with their pants down? *Forum,* pp. 12-22.

Coleman, L. (1986b, July). Has a child been molested? A psychiatrist argues for reforms in the way child sexual abuse cases are investigated. *California Lawyer,* pp. 15-18.

Coleman, L. (1987, April 24). Therapists are the real culprits in many child sexual abuse cases. *Oakland Tribune,* p. B6.

Commonwealth v. Dunkle, 602 A.2d 830 (Pa. 1992).

Corwin, M. (1990, September 10). Court ruling forces new look at sex abuse cases. *Los Angeles Times*, pp. A3, A26.

Council of Juvenile Court Judges. (1949). 15 recommendations made by national council in reviewing juvenile court and children's problems. *Juvenile Court Judges Journal, 1,* 19-24.

Curtiss, A. (1992, December 1). Some on ritual abuse task force say satanists are poisoning them; Government: Skeptics scoff at claims that subcommittee is being attacked with diazinon fumes—even in county meetings. *Los Angeles Times,* p. B1.

Dalmolen, D. (1987, June 13). In beeld: Oude Pekela. *Nieuwsblad van het Noorden, 99,* 2.

Davidson, H., Coen, C. P., & Girdner, L. K. (1994). *Establishing ombudsman programs for children and youth: How government's responsiveness to its young citizens can be improved.* Washington, DC: American Bar Association Center on Children and the Law.

de Mause, L. (1974). *The history of childhood.* New York: Psychohistory Press.

De Volkskrant. (1987, June 15). Deskundige ontleedt verhalen misbruikte kinderen in Oude Pekela. *De Volkskrant,* p. 66.

De Volkskrant. (1988, February 1). Roethof beticht psychiater van moralisme. *De Volkskrant,* p. 67.

Dean, J. (1993, September 14). Parents' group names "hit list" in child welfare. *Arkansas Democrat Gazette,* pp. 1B, 4B.

DeFrancis, V. (1968). Child protective services—1967. *Juvenile Court Judges Journal, 19,* 24-30.

District of Columbia Code Annotated § 1-1182.8 (1981).

Donovan, D. M. (1993, January). Repressed abuse [Letter to the editor]. *APS Observer,* p. 32.

Downs, A. (1972). Up and down with ecology—the "issue-attention cycle." *Public Interest, 28,* 38-50.

Dunsmore, R. A., & Dunsmore, L. D. (1993, March 10). Letter to the editor. *Wall Street Journal,* sec. A, p. 15.

Eberle, P., & Eberle, S. (1986). *The politics of child abuse.* New York: Lyle Stuart.

Eberle, P., & Eberle, S. (1993). *The abuse of innocence.* Buffalo, NY: Prometheus.

Elshtain, J. B. (1985, September). Invasion of the child savers: How we succumb to hype and hysteria. *The Progressive, 49,* 23-26.

Emans, R. (1987, June). Abuse in the name of protecting children. *Phi Delta Kappan, 68,* 740-743.

Evans, S. (1991, October 13). Presumed abusive: Parents feel mistreated by the system. *Washington Post,* pp. B1, B7.

Everson, M. D., Boat, B. W., Bourg, S., & Robertson, K. R. (in press). Beliefs among professionals about rates of false allegations of child sexual abuse. *Journal of Interpersonal Violence.*

Faludi, S. (1991). *Backlash: The undeclared war against American women.* New York: Anchor.

Family Rights Committee. (1989, October 15). HRS' child abuse witch hunt: The reign of terror 1974-? [Paid advertisement]. *Tampa Tribune,* pp. 1-3.

Family Rights Committee. (1992, April 14). HRS: Child abuse witch hunt: The rise of fascism in Florida [Paid advertisement]. *New York Times,* Metro section, p. B5.

Felix v. State, 849 P.2d 220 (Nev. 1993).

Finkelhor, D., & Dzuiba-Leatherman, J. (in press). The victimization of children. *American Psychologist*.

Finkelhor, D., Hotaling, G., Lewis, I. A., & Smith, C. (1989). Sexual abuse and its relationship to later sexual satisfaction, marital status, religion, and attitudes. *Journal of Interpersonal Violence, 4*(4), 379-399.

Flango, C. R. (1988). Should central registries investigate anonymous reports? *State Court Journal, 12*, 13, 38.

Flango, V. E. (1991). Can central registries improve substantiation rates in child abuse and neglect cases? *Child Abuse & Neglect, 15*, 403-413.

Florida Statutes Annotated § § 944.31 (1992 Pocket Part).

FMS Foundation Newsletter. (1992, May 1).

Fortune, C. (1986, October 6). Help for abused parents. *McLean's, 99*, 10-12.

Foster Care Act of 1961, 42 U.S.C. § 5113 (Public Law 87-31).

Fralon, J. A. (1987, June 13). Soixante-dix enfants victimes d'un gang organise aux Pays-Bas, Las tristes clowns du "babyporno." *Le Monde, 44*, 12.

Franklin, B. (1988). Wimps and bullies: Press reporting on child sexual abuse. In *NFWO—contactgroep Rechten van het kind* (Vol. 6, pp. 46-79). Ghent: State University of Ghent, Belgian Study and Documentation Center for Rights of Children. (Reprinted in *Social Work and Social Welfare Yearbook 1990, 1*, 1-14)

Freeman, M.D.A. (1989). Cleveland, Butler-Sloss and beyond—How are we to react to the sexual abuse of children? *Current Legal Problems, 42*, 85-133.

Gardner, R. A. (1991). *Sex abuse hysteria: Salem witch trials revisited*. Cresskill, NJ: Creative Therapeutics.

Gardner, R. A. (1992, October 13). [Sonya Live on CNN with several guests, including Richard Gardner].

Gardner, R. A. (1993, February 22). Modern witch hunt—child abuse charges. *Wall Street Journal*, p. A10.

Gelman, D. (1989, November 13). The sex-abuse puzzle: With charges growing, studies raise doubts about child witnesses. *Newsweek*, pp. 99-100.

Gest, T. (1985, April 1). The other victims of child abuse: In the campaign to aid youngsters, the reputations of some parents and teachers are unjustly being ruined. *U.S. News & World Report, 98*, 66.

Goodman, G. S. (1984). Children's testimony in historical perspective. *Journal of Social Issues, 40*, 9-31.

Goodman, G. S. (1993). Fact or fiction? *MacNeil/Lehrer News Hour* [with correspondent Elizabeth Bracken]. National Public Television.

Goodman, G. S., & Bottoms, B. L. (1993). *Child victims, child witnesses: Understanding and improving testimony*. New York: Guilford.

Goodman, G. S., & Clarke-Stewart, A. (1991). Suggestibility in children's testimony: Implications for sexual abuse investigations. In J. Doris (Ed.), *The suggestibility of children's recollections* (pp. 92-105). Washington, DC: American Psychological Association.

Gordon, C. (1985). False allegations of abuse in child custody disputes. *Minnesota Family Law Journal, 2*, 225-228.

Gordon, L. (1988). *Heroes of their own lives: The politics and history of family violence: Boston 1880-1960*. New York: Viking.

Grimm, B. (1992, July-August). Cloak of confidentiality prevents scrutiny of child protective services. *Youth Law News, 13,* 1-6. (Journal of the National Center for Youth Law)

Groningen District Attorney. (1988, January 21). [Unpublished lecture given at a meeting called for parents in Oude Pekela and described in newspapers January 22, 1988].

Groningen Police Tactical Investigation Team. (1988, January 21). [Unpublished lecture given at parents' meeting in Oude Pekela].

Hechler, D. (1988). *The battle and the backlash: The child sexual abuse war.* Lexington, MA: D. C. Heath.

Hechler, D. (1993). Commentary: Damage control. *Child Abuse & Neglect, 17,* 703-708.

Heeney, T. L. (1985, August). Coping with "the abuse of child abuse prosecutions." *The Champion, 9,* 12-17.

Hentoff, N. (1992a, June 16). Pay no attention to the man behind the curtain. *Village Voice, 37,* 22-23.

Hentoff, N. (1992b, December 26). When authorities browbeat children into a lie. *Washington Post,* p. A19.

Herman, J. (1993, March/April). The abuses of memory. *Mother Jones, 18,* 3-4.

Hester, G. (1981). *Child of rage.* New York: Thomas Nelson.

Het Parool. (1988, February 3). Dr. Mik lijdt een beetje aan verstandsvertroebeling. *Het Parool,* 48.

Hilgartner, S., & Bosk, C. L. (1988). The rise and fall of social problems: A public arenas model. *American Journal of Sociology, 94*(1), 53-78.

Hofstede, P. (1988a, February 6). De sjamaan van het noorden. *Haagse Post,* pp. 18-22.

Hofstede, P. (1988b, May 28). Ietsje in Mie's bil. *Haagse Post,* pp. 24-28.

Hollingsworth, J. (1993, July 25). Suffer the children [Review of *The abuse of innocence: The McMartin preschool trial*]. *Tampa Tribune-Times,* Commentary section, p. 6.

Hopkins, E. (1988, January 11). Fathers on trial: Trumped-up charges of child abuse are divorce's ugly new weapon. *New York, 21,* 42-49.

Horn, M. (1993, November 29). Memories lost and found. *U.S. News & World Report, 115,* 52-63.

Howson, R. (1985, August). Child sexual abuse cases: Dangerous trends and possible solutions. *Champion—Journal of Trial Lawyers.*

Idaho v. Wright, 497 U.S. 805 (1990).

Inspector General Act, 5 U.S.C. § 1-12 (1978).

Jones, A. (1993, May). Children of a lesser mom: Women who fail to save their kids from abusive men may be guilty of neglect. But the courts are calling it murder. *Lear's, 6,* 30-32.

Jones, D. P. H., & McGraw, J. M. (1987). Reliable and fictitious accounts of sexual abuse to children. *Journal of Interpersonal Violence, 2,* 27-45.

Jonker, F., & Jonker-Bakker, I. (1991). Experiences with ritualistic child sexual abuse: A case study from the Netherlands. *Child Abuse & Neglect, 15,* 191-196.

Jonker, F., & Jonker-Bakker, I. (1992). Reaction to Benjamin Rossen's investigation of satanic ritual abuse in Oude Pekela. *Journal of Psychology and Theology, 20,* 260-262.

Kleijwegh, M. (1987, July 27). Wij mensen van Oude Pekela zijn veel te nuchter voor massahysterie. *Vrij Nederland, 48,* 9.

Kleijwegh, M. (1989, January 28). "Over relaties met kinderen is men hier zeer bekrompen": De vele deskundigheden van Benjamin Roosen, bachelor. *Vrij Nederland*, 50.

Koeck, P. (1990). *Notaris X*. Leuven: Kritak.

Koopman, K. (1992). *Als ik het vertel dan krijg ik straf, een persoonlijk verhaal over seksueel misbruik van kinderen*. Amsterdam: Van Gennep.

L.A. Star. (1987, March 11). [Back cover].

Lacayo, R. (1987, May 11). Sexual abuse or abuse of justice? Sometimes the accused child molester may be the victim. *Time*, p. 49.

Lanning, K. V. (1987). *Child molesters: A behavioral analysis* (National Center for Missing and Exploited Children in cooperation with the Federal Bureau of Investigation).

Lanning, K. V. (1992). *Investigator's guide to allegations of "ritual" child abuse*. Washington, DC: U.S. Department of Justice, Federal Bureau of Investigation, National Center for the Analysis of Violent Crime.

Lees-Haley, P. R. (1988, April). Innocent lies, tragic consequences. *Trial, 24*, 37-41.

Leiby, J. (1978). *A history of social welfare and social work in the United States*. New York: Columbia University Press.

Louisiana Statutes Annotated § 24:511 (1992 Pocket Part).

Magnuson, E. (1983, September 5). Child abuse: The ultimate betrayal. *Time*, pp. 20-22.

Manshel, L. (1991, July/August). Reporters for the defense in a child abuse case. *Washington Journalism Review, 13*, 16-21.

Mantell, D. (1988). Clarifying erroneous child sexual abuse allegations. *American Journal of Orthopsychiatry, 58*, 618.

Massachusetts General Laws Annotated, chapter 12A, § 7 (1992 Pocket Part).

Masson, J. M. (1984). *The assault of truth: Freud's suppression of the seduction theory*. New York: Farrar, Straus & Giroux.

Mauss, A. L. (1975). *Social problems as social movements*. New York: Lippincott.

McCartney, S. (1987, June 15). Pied piper sex monsters leave village paralyzed with fear: Streets where children dare not play. *The Star* (London).

Meersman, N. (1992, May 15). DCYS likened to KGB during Concord rally. *Manchester Union Leader*, p. 1.

Melton, G. B. (1991). Lessons from Norway: The children's ombudsman as a voice for children. *Case Western Reserve Journal of International Law, 23*, 197-254.

Molema, W. (1987, June 13). Oude Pekela prooi van sensatieschrijvers. *Nieuwsblad van het Noorden, 99*, 35.

Mottl, T. L. (1980). The analysis of countermovement. *Social Problems, 27*(5), 620-635.

Myers, J.E.B. (1992a). *Evidence in child abuse and neglect cases*. New York: John Wiley.

Myers, J.E.B. (1992b, April 28). State legislators target children's social workers. *Sacramento Bee*, p. B5.

Myers, J.E.B. (1993, August). Letter to the editor. *Lear's, 6*, 11.

Myers, J.E.B. (in press). Adjudication of child sexual abuse. *The Future of Children: Child Sexual Abuse, 4*.

Nanninga, R. (1993, July 24). De strijd tegen de satanisten, baby-offers, rituele martelingen door duivelaanbidders, kindermishandeling: Een moderne heksenjacht. *Hervormd Nederland, 49*, 12-15.

Nathan, D. (1993, February 21). Latest pick for AG has a nanny in her past. *Sacramento Bee*, Forum section, p. 3.

National Association of Public Child Welfare Administrators. (1988). *Guidelines for a model system of protective services for abused and neglected children and their families.* (Available from the American Public Welfare Association, 810 First St., N.E., Suite 500, Washington, D.C. 20002-4205)

National Coalition for Child Protection Reform. (1992a). *Introduction: How the war against child abuse became a war against children* (Issue paper 1). Boston: Author.

National Coalition for Child Protection Reform. (1992b). *False allegations: What the data really show* (Issue paper 2). Boston: Author.

National Coalition for Child Protection Reform. (1992c). *Child abuse and poverty* (Issue paper 3). Boston: Author.

National Coalition for Child Protection Reform. (1992d). *How child protective services works* (Issue paper 4). Boston: Author.

National Commission on Child Welfare and Family Preservation. (1990). *A commitment to change.* (Available from the American Public Welfare Association, 810 First St., N.E., Suite 500, Washington, DC 20002-4205)

Nelson, B. (1984). *Making an issue of child abuse.* Chicago: University of Chicago Press.

Ness, C., & Salter, S. (1993, December 26). Bitter debate over recovered memories: Growing number of claims sparks argument on validity. *San Francisco Examiner*, p. 1.

New York Executive Law § 48 (McKinney's Consolidated Laws, 1982).

Nieuwsblad van het Noorden. (1987a, May 13). Peuters in huis gelokt voor sex in Oude Pekela. *Nieuwsblad van het Noorden, 99*, 1.

Nieuwsblad van het Noorden. (1987b, May 14). Politie begon onderzoek kleuters al vorige week. *Nieuwsblad van het Noorden, 99*, 3.

Nieuwsblad van het Noorden. (1987c, May 15). Kleuters in Oude Pekela misbruikt in twee huizen. *Nieuswblad van het Noorden, 99*, 1.

Nieuwsblad van het Noorden. (1987d, May 23). Nog geen harde feiten rond Pekelder kleuters. *Nieuwsblad van het Noorden, 99*, 17.

Nieuwsblad van het Noorden. (1987e, May 25). Officier van Justitie blijft bij verklaring. *Nieuwsblad van het Noorden, 99*, 5.

Nieuwsblad van het Noorden. (1987f, June 6). Vijftig kinderen sexueel misbruikt in Oude Pekela. *Nieuwsblad van het Noorden, 99*, 1.

Nieuwsblad van het Noorden. (1987g, June 11). Roddelpers stort zich op Oude Pekela. *Nieuwsblad van het Noorden, 99*, 3.

Nijenhuis, H. (1988, February 4). Waarheid en fictie botsen na ontucht met kind. *NRC*, pp. 1, 3.

North Carolina General Statutes § 147-64.5 (1991).

NRC. (1987, June 9). Zeventig kinderen seksueel misbruikt, daders niet bekend. *NRC, 18*, pp. 1, 3.

Ohio Revised Code Annotated § 121.41 (1991 Supplement).

Okami, P. (1990). Sociopolitical biases in the contemporary scientific literature on adult human sexual behavior with children and adolescents. In J. Feierman (Ed.), *Pedophilia: Biosocial dimensions.* New York: Springer-Verlag.

Olafson, E., Corwin, D. L., & Summit, R. C. (1993). Modern history of child sexual abuse awareness: Cycles of discovery and suppression. *Child Abuse & Neglect, 17*, 7-24.

Olmstead v. United States, 277 U.S. 438 (1928).

Pelton, L. (1978). Child abuse and neglect: The myth of classlessness. *American Journal of Orthopsychiatry, 48*, 608-617.

Pfohl, S. J. (1977). The "discovery" of child abuse. *Social Problems, 24*, 310-323.

Phylipsen, W. (1987a, June 9). Zeventig kinderen seksueel misbruikt kinderen. *De Volkskrant, 66*, 1, 4.

Phylipsen, W. (1987b, June 10). Voorlichting ouders misbruikte kinderen wordt verbeterd. *De Volkskrant, 66*.

Phylipsen, W., & Tromp, J. (1988, January 22). Misbruik kinderen verbijstert prof. Mik, ibidem. *De Volkskrant, 67*, 3.

Phylipsen, W., & Tromp, J. (1988, January 22). Psychiater onsteld na onderzoek Oude Pekela. *De Volkskrant, 67*, 1.

Rabinowitz, D. (1990, May). From the mouths of babes to a jail cell—child abuse and the abuse of justice: A case study. *Harper's Magazine*, pp. 52-63.

Rabinowitz, D. (1993, February 22). Deception: In the movies, on the news. *Wall Street Journal*, p. A8.

Radbill, S. X. (1987). Children in a world of violence: A history of child abuse. In R. E. Helfer & R. S. Kempe (Eds.), *The battered child* (pp. 3-22). Chicago: University of Chicago Press.

Rhode Island Laws Annotated § 42-73-1 (1993).

Richardson, S., & Bacon, H. (1991). *Child sexual abuse: Whose problem?: Reflections from Cleveland*. Birmingham, UK: Venture.

Roe v. Wade, 410 U.S. 113 (1973).

Rogers, M. L. (1992). The Oude Pekela Incident: A case study of alleged SRA from the Netherlands. *Journal of Psychology and Theology, 20*, 257-259.

Rose, V. M. (1977). Rape as a social problem: A byproduct of the feminist movement. *Social Problems, 25*, 75-89.

Rossen, B. (1989a). Mass hysteria in Oude Pekela. *Issues in Child Abuse Accusations, 1*, 49-51.

Rossen, B. (1989b). *Zedenangst, het verhaal van Oude Pekela*. Amsterdam/Lisse: Swets & Zeitlinger.

Rossen, B. (1989c). Zedenangst in Oude Pekela. *Psychologie, 8*, 10-15.

Rother, L. (1992, April 16). In ad, Florida group says state child agency undermines families. *New York Times*, Metro section, p. B5.

Satanic abuse: Salem revisited [Unsigned editorial]. (1991, August 31). *The Economist, 320*, 23.

Schulman, Ronca, and Bucuvalas, Inc. (1988). *Public attitudes and actions regarding child abuse and its prevention*. Chicago: National Committee for the Prevention of Child Abuse and Neglect.

Shapiro, L., Rosenberg, D., Lauerman, J. F., & Sparkman, R. (1993, April 19). Rush to judgment. *Newsweek*, pp. 54-60.

Sinnema, P. (1989, January 26). Het bedrog van een geleerde pedophiel. *Het Parool*.

Social Security Act of 1935, 42 U.S.C. § 301 et seq.

Souren, A. (1988, February 6). Roethof verdedigt alleen rechten van volwassenen. *De Volkskrant*, p. 23.

Sowell, T. (1992, November 23). Long on claims, short on evidence. *Forbes*, p. 74.

Spector, M., & Kitsuse, J. I. (1977). *Constructing social problems*. Menlo Park, CA: Cummings.

Spencer, J. R., & Flin, R. (1993). *The evidence of children: The law and the psychology* (2nd ed.). London: Blackstone.

Spiegel, L. D. (1985). *A question of innocence.* Parsippany, NJ: Unicorn.

Spiegel, L. D. (1989, January). Child abuse hysteria: A warning for educators. *Education Digest, 54,* 55-58.

Stapleton, C. (1993, May 18). Could the state take your child? *Woman's Day,* pp. 54-58.

State v. Haseltine, 352 N.W.2d 673 (Wis. Ct. App. 1984).

State v. Michaels, 625 A.2d 489 (N.J. Super. 1993).

Summit, R. C. (1988). Hidden victims, hidden pain: Societal avoidance of child sexual abuse. In G. E. Wyatt & G. J. Powell (Eds.), *Lasting effects of child sexual abuse* (pp. 39-60). Newbury Park, CA: Sage.

The Salem epidemic [Unsigned editorial]. (1990, September 3). *National Review, 42,* 14.

Thoennes, N., & Tjaden, P. G. (1990). The extent, nature, and validity of sexual abuse allegations in custody/visitation disputes. *Child Abuse & Neglect, 14,* 151-163.

Tiffin, S. (1982). *In whose best interest? Child welfare reform in the Progressive Era.* Westport, CT: Greenwood.

Trouw. (1988, February 3). Waarom moet Minister naar Oude Pekela? *Trouw, 46,* 2.

Troyer, R. J., & Markle, G. E. (1983). *Cigarettes: The battle over smoking.* New Brunswick, NJ: Rutgers University Press.

Trunk, L., & Stimpel, R. (1987, June 16). Vorsicht vor den Clowns. *Stern.*

U.S. Advisory Board on Child Abuse and Neglect. (1990). *Child abuse and neglect: Critical first steps in response to a national emergency* (U.S. Department of Health and Human Services, Stock No. 017-092-00104-5). Washington, DC: U.S. Government Printing Office.

U.S. Advisory Board on Child Abuse and Neglect. (1991). *Creating caring communities: Blueprint for an effective federal policy on child abuse and neglect* (U.S. Department of Health and Human Services, Administration for Children and Families, Stock No. 017-092-00104-5). Washington, DC: U.S. Government Printing Office.

U.S. Advisory Board on Child Abuse and Neglect. (1993). *Neighbors helping neighbors: A new national strategy for the protection of children* (U.S. Department of Health and Human Services, Administration for Children and Families). Washington, DC: U.S. Government Printing Office.

Van der Meulen, T. (1988, February 12). Gerrit Mik en de aanvallen op zijn Oude Pekela onderzoek: Mijn rapport is heel concreet. *De Tijd, 14,* 10-13.

Victims of Child Abuse Laws. (1988, January-February). Corwin's army: The great leap forward. *Family Advocate, 4,* 1. (Not published by California State VOCAL.)

von Hoffman, N. (1992, September 9). TV sensationalizes child abuse. *Philadelphia Inquirer,* Commentary section, p. 1.

Wakefield, H., & Underwager, R. (1988). *Accusations of child sexual abuse.* Springfield, IL: Charles C Thomas.

Wald, M. (1975). State intervention on behalf of neglected children: A search for realistic standards. *Stanford Law Review, 27,* 985-1040.

Wald, M. (1976). State intervention on behalf of "neglected" children: Standards for removal of children from their homes, monitoring the status of children in foster care, and termination of parental rights. *Stanford Law Review, 28,* 623-706.

Webster's ninth new collegiate dictionary. (1985). Springfield, MA: Merriam-Webster.

Wexler, R. (1990). *Wounded innocents: The real victims of the war against child abuse.* New York: Guilford.

Whalen, J. (1991). Florida abuse registry loses in federal court. *Issues in Child Abuse Accusations, 3,* 228-231.

Whistle-blower paid high price for doing her duty. (1992, December 30). *Daily Telegraph* (London), p. 4.

Whitman, D. (1987, April 27). *U.S. News & World Report, 102,* 39-40.

Wigmore, J. H. (1970). *Evidence in trials at common law.* Boston: Little, Brown. (Original work published 1904)

Wildavsky, A. (1988, July/August). Ubiquitous anomie: Public service in an era of ideological dissensus. *Public Administration Review, 48,* 752-755.

Winschoter Courant. (1987a, May 14). Oude Pekela geschokt. *Winschoter Courant,* p. 3.

Winschoter Courant. (1987b, May 20). Zedendelict in Oude Pekela veroorzaakt ook onrust in Winschoten. *Winschoter Courant.*

Winschoter Courant. (1987c, May 25). Politie over sexueel misbruik kinderen: "Er is wel iets gebeurd in Oude Pekela." *Winschoter Courant.*

Winschoter Courant. (1987d, June 6). Kinkerlokkers in Oude Pekela liepen als clown rond. *Winschoter Courant.*

Winschoter Courant. (1987e, June 10). Affaire (nog) zonder einde in Oude Pekela. *Winschoter Courant, 117,* 1.

Winschoter Courant. (1987f, June 12). Wereldpers stort zich op seksschandaal kleuters. *Winschoter Courant, 117,* 1.

Winschoter Courant. (1987g, June 15). Hoofdofficier Blok over seksschandaal in Oude Pekela: "Geen sprake van massa psychose." *Winschoter Courant, 117,* 1.

Winschoter Courant. (1988a, January 18). Ouders: Justitie en politie hebben tips laten liggen. Opnieuw twijfel over omvang schandaal Oude Pekela. *Winschoter Courant, 118,* 1.

Winschoter Courant. (1988b, October 31). Psycholoog zorgt voor opschudding rond affaire Oude Pekela. Huisarts beticht van kwalijke rol. *Winschoter Courant, 118.*

Wright, L. (1993, May 24). Remembering Satan—Part II. *The New Yorker, 69,* 54-76.

Younas, L. A. (1987). *State child abuse and neglect laws: A comparative analysis, 1985.* Washington, DC: U.S. Department of Health and Human Services, National Center on Child Abuse and Neglect.

Zald, M. N., & Ash, R. (1966). Social movement organizations: Growth, decay and change. *Social Forces, 44*(3), 327-340.

Index

About the Authors

David Finkelhor, Ph.D., is the Codirector of the Family Research Laboratory and the Family Violence Research program at the University of New Hampshire. His latest publications include *Sourcebook on Child Sexual Abuse* (Sage, 1986), a widely used compilation of research on the subject of sexual abuse, and *Nursery Crimes* (Sage, 1988), a study of sexual abuse in day care. He has been studying the problem of family violence since 1977 and has published three other books, *Stopping Family Violence* (Sage, 1988), *License to Rape* (1985), and *Child Sexual Abuse: New Theory and Research* (1984) and more than two dozen articles on the subject. He is coeditor of *Dark Side of Families* (Sage, 1983), *Coping With Family Violence: New Research* (Sage, 1988) and *New Directions in Family Violence and Abuse Research* (Sage, 1988) and is the recipient of grants from the National Institute of Mental Health and the National Center on Child Abuse and Neglect.

John E. B. Myers, J.D., is Professor of Law at the University of the Pacific, McGeorge School of Law, in Sacramento, California. He is the author of *Evidence in Child Abuse and Neglect Cases* (1992), *Legal Issues in Child Abuse and Neglect* (Sage, 1992), and many articles on child maltreatment. His writing has been cited by more than 100 courts, including the U.S. Supreme Court. He is on the faculty of the National Judicial College, the National Council of Juvenile and Family Court Judges, and the National Center for Prosecution of Child Abuse.

Sylvia Pizzini, M.S.W., M.P.A., recently retired after serving 8 years as the Director of the Santa Clara County Department of Family and Children's Services in California. She has worked for more than 30 years in the social services field, most of the time in child welfare administration at both the county and state level, and has been involved in numerous efforts to improve the child welfare system. She was the manager of the California Child Welfare Strategic Planning Project. She is now managing a 4-year federal research project designed to improve administrative practices in child welfare.

Karel Pyck, M.D., is Professor of Child and Adolescent Psychiatry at the Catholic University of Leuven, Belgium. He has published books and numerous articles on a wide range of subjects related to child psychiatry. He became interested in the backlash in Europe when he consulted on a particularly controversial case. Since that time, he has traveled throughout Europe and the United States studying the backlash.

Susan Caylor Steppe, M.S.S.W., is Director of Child Protective Services, Tennessee Department of Human Services. She has more than 18 years of experience in child welfare, including work in the public and private sectors. Her publications include *Investigating Sexual Abuse in Day Care, Fostering the Sexually Aggressive Child,* and *Meeting Life's Challenges: A Youth Worker's Guide to Empowering Youth and Families.*

Charles Wilson, M.S.S.W., is Director of Child Welfare for the Tennessee Department of Human Services. He has worked in public child welfare for more than 21 years. He has authored several articles in professional publications, along with a 1985 monograph on child sexual abuse investigations in day care settings, coauthored with Susan Caylor Steppe; the National Center on Child Abuse and Neglect's publication *The Role of Law Enforcement,* coauthored with Donna Pence; and a new book with Donna Pence, *Team Investigation of Child Sexual Abuse: The Uneasy Alliance* (Sage, 1994). He is a past president of the American Professional

Society on the Abuse of Children and a past vice president of the National Association of Public Child Welfare Administrators. Together with Donna Pence, he is a frequent speaker at national and regional child abuse conferences and symposiums.

Lesley Wimberly is cofounder and the president of California's chapter of Victims of Child Abuse Laws, Inc. (VOCAL), an organization seeking reform in laws and policies regarding child welfare and protection issues. She is also presently the president of the National Association of State VOCAL Organizations, VOCAL's national entity. She has been publicly active for the past decade, serving as an adviser to the California Department of Justice Advisory Board on the Child Abuse Central Index, the Department of Social Services Child Welfare Training Advisory Board, and the Little Hoover Commission's Advisory Committee on Foster Care Reform. She has also served as a state commissioner on the Child Welfare Strategic Planning Commission in Sacramento, California.